Gluten-free
gourmet recipes

WHITE STAR PUBLISHERS

Texts
Maurizio Cusani

Photographs and recipes
Cinzia Trenchi

Editorial director
Valeria Manferto de Fabianis

Editorial coordination
Laura Accomazzo
Federica Romagnoli

Graphic design
Paola Piacco

PREFACE
by Maurizio Cusani

Coeliac disease is an illness that can create many problems before being identified and which, once recognised forces sufferers to radically change their diet, eating habit and lifestyle. Coeliacs can't eat certain types of foods which contain glutens or even traces of this substance, a very widespread combination of lipoproteins found in certain cereals. A lot of foods contain gluten, but many of them can be replaced without making a coeliac feel completely left out or having to make intolerable sacrifices.

The aims of this book are to suggest worthwhile alternatives to the traditional diet, to provide correct information about how coeliac disease affects our bodies, and to offer a few tips about how to prevent accidentally eating food containing gluten, which is a poison for coeliacs. Knowledge of food and its properties is the key factor in treating coeliac disease. Thanks to simple but tasty recipes and a lot of good advice about the best way to use foodstuffs, what we eat can become an ally and help us stay healthy. The information in this book will help improve energy levels, eliminate the symptoms of coeliac disease, and help us reduce or even stop taking medication to offset the effects of the disease. Food, therefore, becomes a cure, and meals a form of natural medicine. This applies even more so if we prepare what we eat in such a way as to satisfy all our senses. Our aim is for the coeliac to find all the flavor and enjoyment possible in alternative foods, and not constantly feel deprived or as if he or she is always making sacrifices due to the disease. It is worth noting that there has been an increase in the number of less severe forms of coeliac disease. These are the somewhat elusive and unusual "gluten intolerances", sometimes also referred to as the "irritable bowel syndrome" typically found in adults. The fact that more intolerances are now being found is probably linked with improved diagnostics but does not rule out the effects of other factors connected with present day foods.

This book aims to help coeliacs and gluten intolerant individuals adapt their diets to their new requirements and still satisfy their palates with new alternative recipes.

CONTENTS

INTRODUCTION

A QUESTION OF TASTE

It is absolutely essential that we eat healthy, natural food to prevent illnesses. This is becoming increasingly difficult in developed countries. We should try to eat as little meat as possible (preferably home raised and not battery farmed) and eat a lot of seasonal fresh fruit and vegetables. We should drink a lot of water, at least 4 pints (2 litres) a day, and even more in the summer. Freshly squeezed fruit drinks are a good way to replace salts lost through sweat. Drinking a lot of water does not make you put on weight or leave you feeling swollen. It takes away pangs of hunger and helps intestinal flow and kidney functions. As we get older, it is important to eat smaller quantities of food and to eat more live cultures such as yoghurt. We should also avoid foods that are mass produced to be sold more easily. It is best not to eliminate cellulose from the diet as being indigestible. These fibres help the digestive system and also prevent constipation. For a long, healthy life, therefore, we need to eat simple, genuine foods such as fruit, pulses, yoghurt, bread and pasta, but we should also allow ourselves the occasional treat such as desserts, fish or a little meat We recommend the use of vegetable fats, like those found in olive oil, instead of animal fats. By reducing your fat intake you also reduce the effects of ageing and help prevent macular degeneration and blindness. A diet that is rich in fruit, vegetables and fish also helps your body and sight function better over time.

Every type of food has its own characteristics of taste, smell and appearance. Every culture, every epoch and every person has its favourite foods, and for a very good reason. We love the foods which, from a psychological point of view, most represent us. Our tastes change in line with our perceptions. Children, for example, change tastes very quickly as they grow, and they can be very whimsical. Adults, on the other hand, are more stable and systematic, not to mention certain elderly people who always eat the same things.

Those individuals who particularly like "sweet" foods are expressing a desire for dependence, an infantile regression and a need for cuddles. Words like "dolcezza" in Italian or "honey" in English are used in those sweet mutterings between lovers and demonstrate the affection they feel for each other. A sudden need for sweets or even just a preference for sweet foods shows a need for love and tenderness.

Those who particularly like salty foods, instead, show a strong desire for independence, as well as awareness and maturity, and the desire to break away from the routine of a "salt-free" life: basically, the stuff that intellectuals are made of. Salt has always been used, not just to add flavor to food but also to preserve it. "You are the salt of the Earth" said Jesus to the Apostles. Intelligent listeners know to take things "with a pinch of salt" while someone who is useless is "not worth his salt".

The word "spicy" is often associated with works of art, books or histories that have a sexual background. Those individuals who prefer or appreciate spicy food are hiding a desire for sexual transgression or perhaps curiosity.

In the same way, a delicate, pure and tender soul prefers similarly delicate food, whereas a more earthy, energetic and forceful person will show a preference for hard and raw foods. The desire for raw meat in particular is a sign of strength and aggression.

Those individuals who prefer cold foods are expressing a sense of detachment and indifference, while those who like hot food and drinks show a desire for affection, warmth and comfort.

In ancient Roman times, sweet and sour tastes were much appreciated (e.g. pickled cucumbers, marinated fish, *garum*, etc.), as they are in Chinese cuisine today. Many pregnant women crave these tastes, as if they were caught in the throes of a battle between the sweetness and bitterness of life itself.

The desire to eat something with a sharp taste such as a lemon, which is by no means unusual in some young people, expresses the desire to accelerate time itself, to grow up quickly and to be free. A preference for bitter tastes (e.g. bitter herbs) is usually shown by individuals who are afraid of letting go and want to stay where they are "to the bitter end". Alcoholic drinks with a bitter taste help others digest things that "they can't hold down".

When choosing an alcoholic drink, young people and those aspiring to be young, prefer light, sparkling, fruity, white wines. Spumante wines and champagne create an image of frivolity and the desire to have fun. Traditionalists and conservative-minded individuals, on the other hand, prefer red wines, strong tea and smoked foods. A preference for strong, red and often expensive wine (Barolo, Recioto, Brunello, Sassicaia and the like) indicates strength of character and a desire to dominate. In other words, tell me what you like to eat – and drink– and I'll tell you who you are.

Conversely, in food intolerances there is a deeply personal and symbolic link with the food the system refuses.

THE DIGESTIVE APPARATUS AND THE INTESTINES

Food turns into energy thanks to digestion, and the first stage of digestion takes place in the mouth. It is better to eat and chew slowly: the more saliva there is present, the better some digestive processes work, and the lower the risk of overloading the gastrointestinal system.

The digestive process has four main stages: ingestion, enzymatic digestion, absorption and assimilation. Metaphorically speaking, these stages can be compared, in the brain, to paying attention, reflecting, memorising and putting a principle into action. Just as the digestive process produces faeces, the brain generates thoughts. We know its wrong to retain faeces and the same applies to retaining and allowing thoughts to build up without taking action. All the diseases of the digestive apparatus are, in a metaphorical sense, connected with the practical problems we run into in our day to day lives.

The digestive apparatus introduces, digests and re-absorbs the main nutrients in food, and gets rid of what remains through the faeces. This process involves the following organs, in this order: the mouth, pharynx, oesophagus, stomach, small intestine (duodenum, jejunum and ileum), large intestine (caecum, colon and rectum) and finally the anal canal. The surface structures of the digestive apparatus have to withstand the action of digestive enzymes and maintain correct absorption, defence and hormonal activities with the help of normal floral bacteria. There are also smooth muscle structures that are governed by an autonomic involuntary nerve system which helps the progress of food through the system (peristalsis), by contracting and dilating the digestive tract as required.

Food is physically broken down into small pieces by the teeth and then attacked by saliva. The food bolus then passes into the pharynx and oesophagus. Contractions by these organs force the cardia to open and push the bolus into the stomach. The epithelium of the stomach secretes gastric juices and hydrochloric acid, but its main purpose is to absorb proteins. This process can last 3 or 4 hours. The food, transformed into chyme, can force open the pyloric sphincter and reach the first section of the small intestine, i.e. the duodenum. The small intestine connects the stomach and the large intestine. The small intestine measures from 6 to 8 metres and is split into the duodenum, jejunum and ileum; the small intestine is followed by 2 metres of large intestine, that is split into the caecum, the colon (ascending, transverse and descending) and the rectum. Digestive secretions are released in the small intestine from organs such as the liver, the gall bladder and the pancreas, which deliver their products into the duodenum. The digestive process is completed here, thanks to the action of bile (which emulsifies fats), pancreatic juice (composed of amylase, trypsin and lipase enzymes), and intestinal juice (containing the enzymes that complete the digestion, transforming the various nutritive ingredients into amino acids, glucose, fatty acids and glycerol). The small intestine has a slightly rough surface due to the presence of numerous villi. These extensions of the mucus serve to absorb the main nutrients. With their finger-like shape, these villi significantly increase the surface area available for the absorption of nutrients. As coeliac disease strikes the villi, it is all too easy for a sufferer to be affected by a lack of the most important nutrients.

WHAT IS COELIAC DISEASE?

The term coeliac comes from the ancient Greek word *koilía* which means "hollow" or "belly", referring to the fact that this disease manifests itself in a very characteristic way with a swollen or pronounced belly. It is basically a permanent intolerance to gliadin or gluten, a combination of vegetable lipoproteins derived from two different types of protein, glutamine and proline.

In reality, glutamine and proline are found in all cereals, but only some cereal flours can produce gluten, which, it should be noted, is not present in flours and is only created after flour is mixed with water: the protein bonds that go to make gluten are only produced when kneaded dough.

Gluten is produced in numerous cereals: wheat (common and durum), barley, rye, spelt, triticale and kamut. Well worth noting is that wheat proteins are made up of 80% gluten, and that the level in durum wheat is higher than that found in common wheat. Corn, millet, sorghum and rice, on the other hand, are gluten-free. There are also other products with similar uses, such as amaranth, quinoa and buckwheat, that are gluten-free simply because they aren't cereals. Other foods such as pulses, fruit, and starchy vegetables like potatoes, tapioca and chestnuts, are also gluten-free. Oats should be mentioned as a separate issue, as coeliacs, in theory at least, are intolerant to them. However, if oats are consumed in small quantities, they can be easily digested. According to some studies, if pure oats – i.e. oats which have not be contaminated by gluten during processing – were introduced into the system, they would do no harm to over 99% of coeliacs. Unfortunately, however, it is by no means easy to be sure that oats are in fact uncontaminated, and for this reason are best avoided by coeliacs.

Any foods containing cereals with gluten are toxic for coeliacs, as they cause mild or severe damage to the small intestine. This damage tends to reverse in the initial stages of the disease when the toxic substances are eliminated from the diet. If allowed to continue, they can cause significant harm

Treating the disease, therefore, means more than just excluding common foods like bread, pasta, biscuits and pizza from the diet. It means eliminating even the smallest traces of gluten. This involves a serious degree of commitment and a steep learning curve about what is or is not permitted, as consuming even small amounts of gluten can cause reactions of a differing degree of severity.

Saucepans and cooking utensils that have been in contact with gluten in the past can no longer be used, as even the smallest remaining trace of gluten can cause a relapse of the disease. Coeliacs must therefore only eat foods that have been prepared in a safe, protected environment. This rule also applies when eating out in restaurants or as guests.

A fillet of frozen fish might appear the perfect dish for a coeliac, but if the same company also produces breaded fish (coated with a crispy layer of breadcrumbs containing traces of gluten) that travel along the same conveyor belt before being packaged, this simple contact can also contaminate the fillet. This means that, before a coeliac can eat such a fillet, it must be thoroughly washed under running water, something that is not normally done.

The same applies if the corn flour used in products for coeliacs is processed in the same blender used for wheat: it is obvious that traces of wheat, and therefore gluten, will also be present in the corn products. The creation of gluten-free products must therefore be kept completely separate from other processes.

In addition to accidental contamination, we also have the fact that gluten is used as a thickener in sauces, jams, salami, flavorings, creams, ice-creams, various seasonings, medicines, food additives, cocoa butter, and so on.

A food can only be considered gluten-free, i.e. contamination-free, if the percentage of gluten content is less than 20 parts per million (ppm). Nowadays, gluten test kits are available that can detect readings of less than 32 ppm, but new methods are being investigated that should be able to detect readings as low as 0.006 ppm. At present, food packages with a symbol showing a crossed-out ear of corn guarantee a gluten content of less than 20 ppm. The elimination of gluten from the diet will offer coeliacs perfect health, but will not remove the root cause of the problem. There is no option but to completely abolish the intake of the these vegetable proteins for ever.

Coeliac disease was discovered from observations made by a Dutch paediatrician, Willem Karel Dicke, who had noticed clinical improvements in some of the patients he was treating. Due to the lack of food during WWII, these patients had existed on a diet of potatoes, as they had not been able to find bread or wheat products in general. Their conditions deteriorated quickly once the hostilities ceased and they went back to their previous diets of food containing gluten. Until about 20 years ago, coeliac disease was mainly seen as a relatively rare paediatric illness.

It has instead been shown that this disease is not just affecting more and more people, but is also striking adults, frequently creating an intolerance that until recently was referred to as "irritable bowel syndrome". It is estimated that in Europe, coeliac disease affects 1 out of 100-150 people, whereas gluten sensitivity, or GS, involves about 6% of the adult population; in the USA, it affects 1 out of 133 people (and 1 out of 22 people with a coeliac relative). In other words, more than two million people in all. The ways in which the disease presents are extremely wide-ranging, and can differ subtly.

Gluten intolerance is relatively common in children and adolescents, even if they have not been previously diagnosed with coeliac disease. In these cases, there are other presumed symptoms that are taken into consideration and seen as sufficient to introduce a coeliac disease diet (gluten-free), even if coeliac disease has not been confirmed: such symptoms include intestinal irritability, diarrhoea, weight loss, behavioural disturbances, and a family history of the disease. Overall, predictive identification factors lead the experts to believe that gluten intolerance is associated with non-specific gastrointestinal and behavioural disturbances, and perhaps with the perception of the response to the diet in other family members who think they have coeliac disease: the symptoms of coeliac disease are very non-specific and generic, especially at the onset. There are at least four different forms of coeliac disease: infantile (or typical or traditional or greater); atypical (or lesser or delayed); silent; latent (or potential).

In coeliac disease, the symptoms manifest in the first few months of life. In the most traditional form, the symptoms include arrested development during weaning, diarrhoea and abdominal swelling, fatigue, weight loss, vomiting and temperamental behaviour. Obviously, in coeliac children, the later weaning begins, the later the onset of the symptoms: as the child is weaned off mother's milk, other foods are added to its diet, in which the presence of gluten is inevitable. Subsequently, due to the poor absorption of nutritional substances, the following can occur: avitaminosis, electrolyte deficit (magnesium and potassium), anaemia, aesthenia, loss of appetite, rickets, deficit of coagulation of the blood, and other problems. Thanks to modern diagnostic blood tests, this form of the disease can now be identified at an earlier stage.

The atypical or minor form, in which the intestinal tract would not appear to be particularly involved, manifests frequently with poor absorption of calcium in the bones, anaemia and cutaneous dermatitis. This form often affects short people with symptoms of osteoporosis and rickets, mouth ulcers, muscular cramps and stomach pain.

In silent coeliac disease, there are practically no signs, but there are internal intestinal lesions which can reverse as soon as a gluten-free diet is implemented. In many cases, this form is detected through screening of families in which a member has already been diagnosed as a sufferer of coeliac disease.

In the latent form, the presence of the disease is detected through blood tests but the intestine still appears normal. In such cases, dietary restrictions are not yet needed but the individuals involved must always be monitored.

There are numerous illnesses associated with coeliac disease. It is very important to recognise these associated illnesses as they can provide a valuable response and useful information about a potential simultaneous gluten intolerance that has not yet been identified, and can help to start a gluten-free diet that much sooner. Therefore, by improving the absorption of medicines through the intestinal mucus, it will also be possible to improve the treatment of this disease.

Among the most common diseases are autoimmune forms such as diabetes type 1, rheumatoid arthritis, thyroiditis, Addison's disease (adrenal insufficiency), connective tissue diseases and Sjögren's syndrome, an illness typical to adults in which the skin and mucus dehydrate but that especially manifests as a change in the quality of tears and a subsequent loss of their ability to protect the eyes (individuals who suffer from this syndrome have to use artificial tears). Many children suffering from Down's syndrome or Trisomy 21, which is a congenital chromosomal defect, also suffer from coeliac disease. It is worth remembering that behind many autoimmune diseases which includes coeliac disease, there is an element of hereditary predisposition, and especially the presence of specific haplotypes HLA (DR3, DR4, DQ2 and B8). HLA haplotypes are a series of genetic variants that involve different lymphocytes from patient to patient, and are linked to the possible onset of certain illnesses compared to others.

THE CAUSES

Coeliac disease, also known as gluten enteropathy, tropical sprue or intestinal sprue, is a disease caused by different genetic and environmental factors. The hereditary component is the most important factor and for that reason, it is most often found in family members. There are particular HLA factors found on the membranes of some white corpuscles that are especially important in the formation of coeliac disease. About 80% of coeliac children, for example, present DQ2 as the HLA antigen complex. While the genetic condition is necessary, it is not sufficient to create coeliac disease. There are genetic illnesses in which just one mutation is responsible for the disease, and others in which more genes are involved and where environmental factors, such as food intake, can repress or express them, as none of them alone could generate the disease. This is the case with coeliac disease.

Coeliac disease affects some populations in particular, such as Europeans or Americans of European extraction. The most affected country in Europe is Finland. However, it is only believed that this disease is rarer elsewhere because Asian and African populations consume much less gluten than their European or North American counterparts.

In addition, this disease is found almost twice as often in women. There are therefore hormonal and digestive factors which work alongside genetic elements.

And there's more. Sometimes, the disease first manifests following a surgical procedure, pregnancy, child delivery, a period of mourning, an accident, a trauma, a stay in hospital, or severe stress, or even after a simple viral infection. It has recently been scientifically demonstrated that the disease can start following a common rotavirusinfection, which creates a seemingly banal painful stomach or enteritis.

It is believed that, in genetically predisposed individuals or in those with a family history of the disease, the virus alters the adhesion between intestinal villi cells, with the entry of gluten into the spaces between them, followed by inflammation.

The inflammation activates particular lymphocytes, i.e. the cells that defend the body, and stimulates the production of special anti-bodies which attack not only a particular virus protein to destroy it, but also attack similar gluten proteins, which are digested and found on the surfaces of the intestinal villi cells. Attacking these villi cells sets off cell and villi inflammation and atrophy processes, with a subsequent reduction in their absorption capacity.

The most important environmental factor is the presence of gluten in the intestinal villi. Coeliac disease is thus an autoimmune illness in which anti-bodies and lymphocytes "go mad", as they have been altered by a virus, and attack parts of the body, setting off a chronic inflammatory reaction and the destruction of tissue and its function. The lesions affect the small intestine and particularly the duodenum at the start, followed by the jejunum and ileum.

In children, the villi cells in the small intestine regrow in a period that ranges from three to six months from when the gluten-free diet begins. The same process can take years in adults. As soon as the villi have regrown, they go back to satisfactorily absorbing nutrients and transferring them to the blood, thus dealing with the problem of any lack of nutrition.

Coeliacs, therefore, have special anti-bodies in the blood that normal individuals do not possess and which highlight this autoimmune condition. As a final point, it is not to be excluded that the disease begins more easily in the presence of other autoimmune illnesses or in conditions of extended physical stress.

THE SYMPTOMS

Coeliac disease is a "stealthy" disease with a varying, somewhat strange and volatile pattern of symptoms that changes from person to person. It can simulate a considerable number of intestinal illnesses such as generic intoxication, gastric ulcers, colitis, parasitic diseases and many others.

It frequently strikes at the same time as aesthenia, anxiety, depression, general malaise, halitosis and headache.

The first organ to be affected, especially in children, is the small intestine which, in the presence of gluten, leads inevitably first to inflammation then atrophy. This damage leads to the poor absorption of nutrients. Symptoms include pain, cramps and swelling of the stomach, meteorism and flatulence, diarrhoea (also constipation on rare occasions) and sometimes vomiting.

Diarrhoea is one of the causes of dehydration and poor absorption of nutrients, and is one of the results of poor digestion, which also affects the fats and proteins in foods following the compromising of certain digestive enzymes such as cholecystokinin (which stimulates the contraction of the gall bladder) and secretin. Due to autoimmune mechanisms, many coeliacs can also develop an intolerance to lactose and therefore no longer digest milk products or cheeses. Once gluten is removed from the diet, however, an improvement can be seen in terms of this intolerance. The faeces are often pale, greasy and foul smelling. Children tend to lose weight, to be tired and grow more slowly. Coeliac disease can however also be suspected in people of normal weight or in the obese.

Abdominal pains feel like colitis, and come and go. They are not usually strong or cramp-like, and are caused by large volumes of gas formed by the fermentation of seeds in the colon,which creates swelling in the coils of the large intestine.

Aesthenia, i.e. a feeling of weakness and fatigue, is nearly always present. It is sometimes accompanied by a drop in blood pressure and a lack of potassium and magnesium. There can also be tooth enamel problems due to a deficit in the production of dentine and a delay in the onset of puberty. Also on the subject of the poor absorption of nutrients, a wide ranging set of symptoms can appear: bone pain and fragility, osteoporosis and bones that break easily due to the lack of calcium and vitamin D (which can cause secondary hyperparathyroidism, paraesthesia and muscular pain), anaemia from a lack of iron, anaemia from a lack of folic acid and vitamin B12, deficit in coagulation due to a lack of vitamin K with subsequent micro-haemorrhages, joint pain, tingling in the hands and feet, sometimes anxiety and depression, convulsions, irregular or no menstruation, polyneuropathies caused by the lack of an amino acid known as thiamine, mouth ulcers and a swollen tongue (glossitis), poor night vision (nyc-talopia) due to a lack of vitamin A, and the appearance of an unusual skin rash known as dermatitis herpetiformis.

In other cases, the symptoms are so intangible as to seem non-existent. There is sometimes an increase in the transaminase levels in the liver (known as GOT and GPT) and hyposplenism (reduced functionality of the spleen). All this depends on how long the child was breast-fed, on the type of diet adopted, on the impact of environmental factors, on the degree of stress suffered, on genet-ic factors, and on the individual's predisposition to the disease.

In adults, the demonstration of gluten intolerance takes on an even more elusive late appearance, with wider ranging symptoms. Miscarriages can occur in women and men can become sterile. In certain cases, if the diet is very low in gluten, the symptoms may not even appear.

Different forms of colitis are very common (irritable bowel syndrom), mouth ulcers, hair loss in well defined areas, lack of tooth enamel, and dermatitis her-petiformis, a skin rash that affects about 20% of people suffering from coeliac disease causing severe itching and the appearance of blisters, usually on the el-bows, knees and buttocks. The same areas are more often affected by another form of skin disease, psoriasis. This skin disease can be treated with antibiotics such as Dapsone and cortisones. Most people suffering from dermatitis her-petiformis do not present digestive symptoms associated with coeliac disease.

COMPLICATIONS ASSOCIATED WITH COELIAC DISEASE

Strict adherence to the diet prevents the onset of complications. A coeliac who looks after him or herself and follows the right diet can have a perfectly normal life.

On the other hand, the continuous exposure to gluten caused by a lax diet and/or a late diagnosis can lead to the development of a range of complica-tions associated with coeliac disease. It is these complications that lead to a death rate in adult coeliacs that is almost twice that seen in the general popu-lation of the same age.

In children we see arrested development and delays in puberty, as well as a general insufficiency in intestinal absorption, and subsequent anaemia, avitaminosis, precocious osteoporosis and deficiency syndromes.

In cases of severe complications, coeliac disease can enhance the development of a particular intestinal tumour known as lymphoma. Patients with coeliac disease are 50 to 100 times more likely to develop lymphoma than the general population. This condition can stealthily establish itself in a coeliac under the guise of a gradual worsening of the patient's condition, with symptoms of general malaise, anorexia, weight loss, diarrhoea and fever. Sometimes, especially in young patients, the onset can be rapid and manifest as an intestinal blockage or with acute stomach pain which appears to be appendicitis or an intestinal perforation.

Coeliacs also run a higher risk of developing other tumours of the gastrointestinal apparatus, such as carcinoma of the pharynx, oesophagus, stomach and small intestine.

As a further consequence of the disease, hyposplenism can occur, i.e. a reduced functionality of the spleen. Hypotrophy or atrophy of the spleen affects 30% of adult coeliacs. The significantly reduced volume of the spleen can be seen through an ultrasound scan, and a simple blood test can detect old red blood corpuscles in circulation as they haven't been absorbed by the spleen. This hypofunction reduces the defence capacity of the body and can be accompanied by a pneumococcal infection. It also facilitates the formation of autoimmune diseases.

Chronic jejunum/ileum ulcers can also occur which can lead to bleeding and perforations in the tracts affected. This type of complication can be the manifestation of the onset of an untreated or unrecognised coeliac disease, and is accompanied by a relapse in the patient's condition, with fever, abdominal pain, anaemia and an increase in the number of white corpuscles in the blood.

Neurological complications of coeliac disease can include epilepsy and encephalopathies. Other possible consequences include autoimmune diseases that can be linked to diabetes type 1, diseases of the thyroid, liver and adrenal glands, rheumatoid arthritis, systemic lupus erythematosus, connective tissue disease, Sjögren's syndrome, myocardiopathies and others.

Lastly, we have a variety of poor absorption factors which can cause osteoporosis and fractures, kidney stones (from Calcium oxalate), anaemia, miscarriages and sterility, thyroid alterations, lack of vitamins (avitaminosis with a lack of folic acid and vitamins A, B12, D, E and K), neuropathies, alopecia and dermatitis, mouth ulcers, vascular and liver diseases, changes in tooth enamel, dry eyes due to hypolacrimia, oedema from lack of protein in the blood, and tingling in the hands and feet.

It is also essential to exclude the presence of parasitic diseases such as giardiasis.

The psychological complications are less important and tend to come from a sense of being different from others. These feelings are more common in adolescent coeliacs and can lead to anxiety and depression.

Depending on the complications that occur (and the gender of the patient), consultation with one of the following specialists may be necessary: gynaecologist, neurologist, rheumatologist, dentist, endocrinologist, dermatologist or a psychologist. The referring doctor, however, will continue to be the internist or paediatrician, depending on the patient's age, as will the gastroenterologist and the dietician.

DIAGNOSES

It is quite common practice to begin a gluten-free diet even before coeliac disease has been confirmed. This can be one of the factors that causes a complication in the manifestation of symptoms and a delay in a definite diagnosis. Indeed, it has recently been shown by studies that, while on the one hand it is true that staring a gluten-free diet is an effective way of obtaining information about a suspected case of coeliac disease (for example by providing evidence about whether the change in diet causes the symptoms to disappear), it is equally true that abstinence from gluten for more than a year, without trying other diagnostic methods in the meantime to confirm the disease, can cause long-term damage to the intestinal villi. This is due to the fact that in such cases, abstinence is not always rigorous (as opposed to the case of a confirmed coeliac). This is because the individual does not feel ill and is therefore less rigid about adhering to the diet. Moreover, there is little the doctor can do, as he or she has no way of knowing with certainty whether or not the patient is abstaining from gluten in absolute terms.

To complicate the matter further is the fact that the onset of the disease is increasingly atypical in adults, and that adolescents, even if confirmed coeliacs, tend to easily "overlook" the diet, sometimes subconsciously.

Even if we ignore these facts, the diagnosis of coeliac disease can in any case be very complicated, as most of the symptoms are very similar to other diseases. As a result, this disease is far from easy to recognise on the first examination of the patient. It can also be underestimated, and taken to be a simple case of anaemia or poor digestion.

Any examination of the faeces is often inconclusive. While it is true that the faeces of a coeliac are greasy (steatorrhea), this condition also applies to many other intestinal illnesses caused by poor absorption.

A more reliable method is to examine the anti-bodies which, perhaps through the action of a virus, develop to combat the inflammation caused by gluten. The most frequent are EMAs (Anti-Endomysial antibodies), AGAs (Antigliadin antibodies) and TGAs (Anti-transglutaminase antibodies), and further tests are currently being developed (antireticulin antibodies and anti-jejunal antibodies). The EMAs and AGAs are the best indicators, as TGAs can create many false positives. Patients with high levels of EMA and AGA in the blood have a 95% probability of being coeliac. This research, however, must be performed in the presence of a diet that also involves the use of gluten.

Some coeliac diseases are seronegative, which means that more invasive measures have to be taken. The diagnosis of coeliac disease can only be confirmed with absolute certainty via a biopsy of the duodenum or jejunum performed by gastroduodenoscopy. This procedure involves introducing a thin tube (the endoscope) through the patient's mouth then into the stomach and small intestine to remove a sample.

This sample may show lesions that are typical of coeliac disease, characterised by flattening and atrophy of the villi and by the infiltration of lymphocytes. If the results of the biopsy are positive, it is appropriate to screen all first degree relatives.

The results of the biopsy can however be invalidated by the possible presence of viral gastroenteritis, which is characterised by a completely different set of symptoms. The same can apply to allergies to milk and soya, but these are somewhat rare and tend to show at an early age.

Even though allergies and food intolerances can cause similar symptoms (swollen stomach, skin rashes, breathing difficulties, abdominal pain, etc.), the underlying causes are very different. An allergy is the body's immediate reaction involving the activation of specialised anti-bodies when faced with exposure to an allergenic substance (this exposure can be through inhalation, contact or by assumption of a food). An intolerance, instead, is the sum result of a number of simultaneous factors and involves the lymphocytes in the blood. Even though both cases involve a hereditary and constitutional predisposition, in allergies the hereditary factors are more powerful than in intolerances.

The number of intolerances is increasing for different reasons, which include a monotonous diet, the use of frozen and canned foods, the abuse of medicines/drugs, drinking too little water, and physical/psychological stress. One good way of treating intolerance is to gradually reintroduce the suspected substances after a period of abstinence, ranging from two months to one year. There are also different intolerances to additives and preservatives, especially to those used in the preparation of ready-meals and snacks. The most common involve aspartame, benzoic acid, monosodium glutamate, polysorbate 80, potassium nitrite and nitrate, saccharin, ascorbic acid (vitamin C), sodium sulfite and sodium metabisulfite.

HOW TO COPE WITH COELIAC DISEASE

A proper diet is the key factor in coping with coeliac disease. Total abstinence from contact with gluten stops the disease, and can reverse intestinal alterations and hinder the development of potential complications. There is no choice but to avoid gluten for life, with no exceptions.

Unfortunately, wheat is one of the most commonly found prepared foods, so the use of specific gluten-free products becomes almost inevitable. Nowadays, these products can be found not just in specialised shops, but also in well stocked supermarkets.

The main problems are usually connected with taking gluten accidentally. In restaurants, for example, dishes might be served that, while gluten-free, have not been cooked in pans set aside for that purpose (or plates and utensils used during cooking that have previously been in contact with gluten), and therefore will inevitably still have traces of gluten.

It is also important to remember that wheat starch is very often used as a thickener and preservative, even in pharmaceutical products. You must always read the "excipients" or "ingredients" section before taking any medicinal product.

You also need to be careful when ordering an espresso coffee, as it may have been contaminated with barley. Do not drink "normal" beer. Have a gluten-free one instead. The same rules apply to many spices, icing sugar, precooked foods and items that have previously had flavorings added, such as fruit yoghurt and many industrially manufactured drinks.

If the diet is followed properly, this type of therapy will be sufficient in about 80% of cases. In the few cases that remain, i.e. those with refractory coeliac disease, "suppressive" therapy is called upon to control the activity of the auto-antibodies against the small intestine. It is vital in all cases to check that no complications develop from the poor intestinal absorption of nutrients.

It is therefore best to monitor for any possible deficit of iron and vitamins which can lead to anaemia, and of calcium and vitamin D which can lead to osteoporosis and thyroid problems. It is for exactly this reason that all coeliacs should be examined by a hospital doctor and gastroenterologist at least once a year and have blood tests taken.

The most gluten a coeliac can take in food is 20 ppm (parts per million). Once over this threshold, it becomes toxic. European legislation has established that this is the limit under which a food can be classified as gluten-free and which allows the manufacturer to display the crossed-out ear of wheat logo on the product label.

Another type of therapy is currently being tested that involves a vaccine against rotaviruses for use in early infancy. It would appear that these viruses are the main source of the disease in genetically predisposed individuals. At the moment, however, this therapy is still not practicable.

SENSITIVITY TO GLUTEN OR IRRITABLE BOWEL SYNDROME

Irritable bowel syndrome has been well known for many years and is characterised by a particularly sensitive intestine. Symptoms include stomach cramps after eating, with abdominal swelling, meteorism, flatulence, and diarrhoea alternating with constipation. The abdominal pain comes mainly from alterations to the intestinal flora, at the same time as poor small intestine functioning, and is accompanied by chronic local inflammation.

This syndrome is very common, particularly in industrialised countries, and affects nearly one out of five Italians, i.e. 20% of the population. It is even more widespread in Mexico and Brazil where it affects more than 40%. Japan and India are less afflicted. Women are affected by gluten sensitiviy (or GS) almost twice as much as men.

The causes behind irritable bowel syndrome vary, and can include: physical and psychological stress (mourning, separation, divorce, accidents, losing a job, etc.), which alter the balance between the digestive system's sympathetic and parasympathetic nervous system; prior diseases of the digestive system, such as gastrointestinal dysentery (from shigella, *campylobacter* and similar) or the surgical removal of intestinal tracts; a diet that is rich in refined cereals and saturate fats or that is free of fibre or trace elements; several hormonal alterations (for example, it is known that women with this syndrome suffer more during menstruation); and lastly, hereditary/genetic predisposition.

The treatment for irritable bowl sydrome is personalised, as each individual needs a therapy which responds to the characteristics of his or her specific case. For example, for some it is important to limit the amount of milk, while for others it is vegetables, and for some, probiotics are very useful.

However, it has only recently been discovered that the so-called "irritable bowel sydrome" is none other than a delayed, typically adult, hypersensitivity to gluten. While coeliac disease is a true autoimmune disease in which the antibodies attack the intestinal villi, in the case of gluten sensitivity, an innate immune mechanism kicks in, triggered especially by the modern diet, not to mention by gluten itself.

Most cases of GS still remain under-diagnosed or mistaken due to the presence of a volatile and often elusive symptomatic picture. Another reason for this is the almost total lack of appropriate diagnostic equipment. The diagnosis of GS must first of all exclude the presence of gastrointestinal tumours, ulcerative colitis, Crohn's syndrome, anatomic alterations of the intestinal tract, and metabolic or hormonal alterations.

GS improves after defecation and is often associated with an alteration in the rhythm of evacuating the bowels and with changes in the consistency of the faeces, which are greasy and foul-smelling.

GS can be split into four groups depending on the consistency and characteristics of the faeces: a) hard, round shaped faeces in patients suffering from constipation; b) individuals who do not evacuate the bowels more than three times a week and often after great effort (frequently with the use of various types of laxatives) and always have the feeling of not having evacuated enough; c) soft liquid faeces with traces of mucus in individuals who evacuate two or three or more times a day with urgency; d) faeces which alternate between soft and hard rounded shapes, with alternating episodes of diarrhoea and constipation, sometimes even in the same day; e) long periods of constipation, alternating with diarrhoea (the latter are the most volatile forms). Each of these four groups shares about 25% of the GS cases found in clinical practice.

GS can be easily diagnosed if the above events persist for at least six months running. In such cases, meteorism is always present, as is a very contracted belly at the colon that, mainly on the left side, is painful to the touch. Often, however, other diseases of the intestinal tract have to be excluded, such as diverticulosis, infections and tumours. The use of diagnostic methods such as colonoscopy may also be necessary.

The intimate metabolic mechanisms which can support GS are still almost unknown. For example, it has only recently been discovered that vitamin A and its metabolites, which are extremely useful as regards the sight and have benefits for the skin, in effect enhance GS.

In a stressed intestinal environment, retinoic acid, which is a derivative of vitamin A, promotes local inflammation instead of preventing it. This helps explain why some individuals suffering from juvenile acne who use vitamin A as part of the cure, begin to manifest digestive symptoms like those found with GS as side effects, while at the same time displaying an intolerance to gluten.

We still know very little about how food intolerances form over time, despite their rapid increase in the industrialised western world.

It is particularly important to investigate foods that are associated with symptoms, and to completely exclude them. In many cases, it is best to use anti-spasm and pain killing medicines, not to mention anxiolytics (e.g. bromides) if the patient complains of a particular state of anxiety/depression which only worsens the existing symptoms.

Fructoses such as sorbitol and mannitol are useful for helping treat diarrhoea and should always be accompanied by an increase in water/liquid intake.

For constipation, natural tamarind and plum based laxatives are best.

Meteorism can be effectively countered by eliminating gluten, eating more fibre and taking probiotics (live bacteria which improve the state and effectiveness of the intestinal flora). If the intestinal flora is in a state of equilibrium, this hinders the formation of pathogenic bacteria, normalises the function of the intestinal villi, and enhances the proper absorption of vitamins and trace elements. The most commonly found probiotics are lactobacillus and bifidobacterium. These can withstand the hydrochloric acid in the stomach and the duodenal enzymes to reach the intestine active and proliferate there. Probiotics are especially useful during periods both of constipation and diarrhoea. They are also essential during all antibiotic therapies.

While natural white yoghurt can be an excellent alternative to the probiotics available in the shops, you need to be careful that it does not contain additives (which it often does, and which ferment) and as a precaution, do not not overindulge.

PROHIBITED CEREALS

The following cereals are not allowed.

Barley (barley coffee, biscuits, soups, pastas, bread, pizzas, breadcrumbs, etc.)

Farik or kamut or green Egyptian wheat (flours, biscuits, Danish toasts, etc.)

German or Greek green wheat (bread and pizzas, breadsticks, soups, piadine, etc.)

Oats, as they often contain malt and/or other cereals (soups, cereal yoghurts, ready-to-eat foods, etc.)

Rye (bread, breadsticks and rye crackers, etc.)

Seitan (wheat gluten, kofu, some vegetarian seasonings, most soy sauces)

Spelt (soups, bran, malt, flours for cakes and biscuits, etc.)

Triticale, a wheat and rye hybrid (flours, biscuits, Danish toasts, etc.)

Wheat (durum and bread wheat, corn flakes, wheat germ, pasta, bread, pizza, breadcrumbs, etc.)

PROHIBITED FOODS

The following foods are not allowed.

Battered dessicated fruits (dried figs, etc.)
Battered dried figs
Battered foods (battered vegetables, etc.)
Beer
Biscuits made from prohibited cereals
Bran made from prohibited cereals
Bread crostini
Bread made from prohibited cereals
Breadcrumbs made from prohibited cereals
Breaded and battered vegetables
Breaded foods (fish and meat cutlets, ready-to-eat meals with breaded cheeses, etc.)
Breadsticks made from prohibited cereals
Bulgur
Cakes made from prohibited cereals
Chocolate with cereals
Confectionery made from prohibited cereals
Couscous
Cracked wheat
Crackers made from prohibited cereals
Creams made from prohibited cereals

Crêpes made from prohibited cereals
Croquettes made from prohibited cereals
Danish toast made from prohibited cereals
Drinks containing barley (barley coffee, barley mixes, soluble barley, etc.)
Drinks containing malt (malt whisky, cream liqueurs, etc.)
Drinks containing rye
Extract of malt from prohibited cereals
Filled pastas (tortellini, ravioli, etc.)
Flakes made from prohibited cereals (corn flakes)
Flours made from prohibited cereals
Focacce made from prohibited cereals
Foods cooked in sauces or sauces thickened with prohibited flours (béchamel, etc.)
Foods with breadcrumbs (hamburgers, dumplings)
Forbidden cereal starches
Frozen fish to be fried (mixed fried fish, fish fingers, etc.)
Malt
Meat or fish cutlets

Mother yeast or natural yeast
Muesli
Oatmeal drinks
Pastas (spaghetti, tortiglioni, tagliatelle, etc.)
Pastries made from prohibited cereals
Piadine
Pizza
Pizzoccheri (short tagliatelle)
Polenta taragna (if the buckwheat flour is mixed with wheat flour)
Porridge
Potato gnocchi
Pre-cooked frozen fish (paella, surimi)
Puff pastries made from prohibited cereals
Ready-to-eat meals with breaded cheeses
Savoury pastries
Semolina

Semolina gnocchi
Semolinas made from prohibited cereals
Soluble coffee or coffee surrogates containing barley or malt
Soups made from mixed cereals
Soups with cereals
Tabouli
Taralli
Vegetable fibres from prohibited cereals
Vegetables with cereals (soups and frozen minestrones)
Vodka
White bread for toast made from prohibited cereals
Yoghurt with biscuits
Yoghurt with cereals
Yoghurt with malt

RISKY FOODS

The following foods are not prohibited, but run the risk of having been contaminated with gluten during the production process. This means you need to be careful and always check their provenance.

Anchovy paste
Barley drinks
Beer
Biscuits
Bonbons
Brand name popcorn
Cakes
Candied fruit
Candied sweets
Caramelised fruit
Cereal oils
Cheese slices
Cheese spreads
Chemical yeast
Chewing gum

Chocolate and hazelnut spreads
Chocolate bars
Chocolate drink powders
Cocoa powder
Cold tea
Condensed milk
Cooked ham
Creamy yoghurts
Curry
Drink powders (tea, coffee)
Flavored cream
Flavored vinegars or non-DOP balsamic vinegar
Flavorings
Flour for polenta

Flours of permitted cereals
Frozen or instant mashed potato
Fruit based drinks
Fruit juices
Glazed fruit
Home made or brand name ice cream
Homogenised cheese products
Homogenised fruit products
Homogenised meat products
Hot dog sausages
Icing sugar
Jams and preserves
Jellys
Ketchup
Light butter
Margarine
Marron glacés
Marzipan
Mayonnaise
Meat extracts for making stock
Meat or vegetable stock cubes or liquids
   for making stock
Melted cheeses
Milk shakes
Miscellaneous creams
Miscellaneous desserts
Miscellaneous mousses
Miscellaneous sweets
Mortadella
Mostarda
Mustard
Nectars and fruit juices
Non-defined seasonings
Oatmeal drinks
Paté
Potato crisps
Powdered milk
Pre-fried frozen potatoes
Pre-packed meats

Preserved fish
Preserved vegetables
Puffed and flaked cereals
Ready-to-bake cakes
Ready-to-eat dishes with pre-cooked
   frozen vegetables
Ready-to-eat pesto
Ready-to-eat polenta
Ready-to-eat risottos
Ready-to-eat sauces
Ready-to-eat, pre-cooked or tinned meat
   or fish dishes
Salt additives
Sauces, including soy
Sausages
Sausages and salami
Soluble coffees
Soups made from mixed cereals
Speck ham
Spray cream
Starches of permitted cereals
Starches of permitted cereals
Syrups for drinks and slushes
Tacos
Tapioca
Tinned pork products
Tofu
Torrone
Tortillas
UHT cream
Vegetable fibres
Vodka
Wafers and gallette
Whipped cream
Whisky that is not Scottish
Yoghurt with additives
Yoghurt with fruit
Yoghurt with malt

PERMITTED FOODS

The following foods are permitted as they do not contain gluten.

Amaranth
Bee pollen
Buckwheat
Butter
Coffee
Cognac
Corn
Cream
DOP balsamic vinegar
DOP cured ham
DOP cured pork fat
Eggs
Extra-virgin olive oil
Fish (all fresh varieties)
Fresh and dried fruit and fruit
  syrups (all)
Fruit juices with no additives
Grappa
Greek and natural yoghurt
Herbs (all)
Honey
Honey vinegar
Infusions
Kanten (seaweed)
Meat (all)
Milk and milk products

Millet
Mushrooms (all edible types)
Non malt Scotch whisky
Olive oil
Pork lard
Potatoes
Pulses (all)
Quinoa
Raw liquorice
Rice
Royal jelly
Rum
Seaweed (all)
Shellfish (all fresh varieties)
Sorghum
Sparkling drinks with no additives
Spices (all)
Sugars (all)
Tapioca
Tea
Teff
Tequila
Vegetable oils (not cereal oils)
Vegetables (all)
Wine
Wine vinegar

THE IDEAL WEEK

In the future there will probably be effective therapies to treat coeliac disease or vaccines or drugs that can be used on a continual basis with no side effects. Maybe genetic engineering, which is presently making great advances, will find a solution to the problem. Nowadays however, the only practicable way forward for a coeliac to ensure a healthy life is to abstain completely from gluten and adopt a suitable diet. A recent study carried out at Harvard in the USA compared two different groups of children with a mean age of 9 (i.e. their ages ranged from 3 to 17). The members of both groups followed a gluten-free diet but those in the first group only followed this diet once their coeliac disease had been definitely diagnosed. Those in the second group went ahead with the diet before such confirmation was available. Obviously, a mild intolerance of gluten was suspected in all of the children (though it is also very common in adolescents) based on non-specific symptoms such as episodes of diahorrea, weight loss, irritability and a family history of coeliac disease. The results of the study showed an improvement in the symptoms of both groups but also confirmed how important it is to have an accurate diagnosis. In practice, it is essential to start with a correct diet and at the same time start the diagnostic procedures to be absolutely sure that coeliac disease is the root of the problem.

The reason this is important is that the diet must be followed with the consistency that comes from knowing about the disease. There must be no lapses or moments of weakness and with good scheduling and diet rotation, any lack of nutrients will be avoided. The aim of this book is not to take over the role of the doctor treating a coeliac or to suggest the correct diet, instead its intent is to help lovers of good food who suffer from the disease to lead a better life and enjoy a tasty varied diet through new appetizing but healthy recipes. This book will show how the coeliac, with the right guidance, can get the best out of the range of permitted foods and once again enjoy sitting down to a meal bursting with all the flavor and aromas that seemed a thing of the past. Below is an example of how to organise a well planned diet for a week.

MONDAY
BREAKFAST – 7.30
A good breakfast is essential, especially on Mondays, for recharging your energy levels and for starting the week well. We recommend English Breakfast tea with meliga (cornmeal) biscuits, cured pork fat and eggs. Tea bags are best as there is less risk of the tea having had aromatising powders added. The eggs must be fresh, absolutely not powdered or aromatised as there is the chance of contamination; you can eat the whole egg (or, if you prefer, just the yolk). The cured pork fat too (or bacon as an alternative that goes perfectly with eggs, as long as there are no weight problems) must be from a safe provenance. Why not some real DOP pork fat from Colonnata?

BREAK – 10.00

Starting the day is never easy, especially Mondays. We recommend a few biscuits from home or corn breadsticks at your break.

LUNCH – 12.30

For lunch we suggest a single serving of food that is not too heavy but has a high energy content such as courgettes and slices of salmon. You could prepare courgette and salmon rolls or simply grilled courgettes with a slice of salmon. The courgettes are very easily digested while the salmon is rich in proteins and omega-3 fatty acids which are now considered real life-savers and have excellent anti-aging properties. If you fancy, you could also have lettuce as a side dish.

SNACK – 16.00

The working day is drawing to a close but you still need one last effort. Something tasty – like potato breadsticks with paprika – can provide you with the energy you need.

DINNER – 20.30

Monday's almost over: no engagements this evening, stay at home and relax. Your digestive system too needs time to recover from any excesses at the weekend so you should give it a break and not overburden it. The perfect dinner would be bite-sized pieces of turkey with lettuce and an apple to finish off. Turkey is a prized white meat that is rich in proteins and accompanying it with lettuce facilitates digestion by the intestinal villi. Then, as you know, an apple a day... Remember that apples, like pears, do not ferment in the stomach so you can eat them after meals. All other fruits must be eaten before other foods, especially in the evening.

TUESDAY

BREAKFAST – 7.30

A few chocolate and cofee Krumiri biscuits and a small coffee: for today we suggest a very quick breakfast but in general it is best not to eat in a hurry without even sitting down.

BREAK – 10.00

A few slices of rice flour bread with sesame and potato starch. Chew very slowly and work in the office will instantly take on a new meaning.

LUNCH – 12.30

A cheese farinata with chickpeas and Gorgonzola, a nice hot dish. Let's not forget that chickpeas are the third most commonly consumed pulse in the world after beans and soy. They contain a lot of proteins, amino acids and fibre but just 6% of sugars and fats. They are rich in potassium, phosphorus, calcium and magnesium as well as vitamins E, C, K and B-complex vitamins. In other words, they're good to eat and good for you.

SNACK – 16.30

A few almond biscuits with almond milk. This is a highly nutritious blend but remember to go easy on the biscuits.

DINNER – 20.30

Begin with a nice bunch of grapes. To show some respect to our digestive rhythms, it is always better to start meals with the foods that are digested the fastest as this prevents fermentation and a swollen stomach. Next, something tasty like quinoa meatballs with sesame seeds and linseeds. This dish is both light and nutritious. Linseeds are also well known for their anti-tumour properties. A dish like this is tasty, light and perfect for a coeliac.

WEDNESDAY
BREAKFAST – 7.30

Blueberry muffins with yoghurt: blueberries are delicious and very useful as they are rich in antacyanosides which are exceptionally efficient anti-oxidants that protect the sight. They also contain hydrocinnamic acid that can neutralise carcinogenic substances that may be produced in the digestive apparatus. Blueberries are also very effective in preventing capillary fragility and all vascular diseases. The yoghurt on the other hand is ideal fro protecting the colon from possible tumours and for keeping the intestinal flora in balance and regulating evacuation of the bowels.

BREAK – 10.00

Two cheese breadsticks with ricotta and brewer's yeast. Just enough to fool your hunger.

LUNCH – 12.30

A rice flour bruschetta with tomato and some Tuscan extra-virgin olive oil but no garlic.

SNACK – 16.30

A couple of meliga (cornmeal) biscuits.

DINNER – 20.30

The perfect dinner would be a first course of vegetarian meatballs with dried fruit (pine nuts, pistachios, sesame seeds or similar), tofu, eggs, aubergines and sweet peppers. The second course would be: cuttlefish stuffed with paprika, chilli and orange. Before your last coffee of the day, we'd suggest a slice of buckwheat cake with corn, rice and pineapple.

THURSDAY
BREAKFAST – 7.30
Tea made with an Earl Grey teabag, a piece of seasonal fruit and a 100 gram tub of natural or plain yoghurt.

BREAK – 10.00
You have to skip your break today for an unplanned office meeting but the occasional fast will do you no harm.

LUNCH – 13.15
To make up for missing your break, have a large satisfying lunch: oven baked celery with cornmeal and cornflour breadcrumbs. As a side dish you could have a mixed dried fruit salad (almonds, pistachios or similar), curly lettuce and chicory. For afters, chestnut starch cakes with rice and chestnut flour: a delicious dessert that more than makes up for the missed snack at break time.

DINNER – 20.30
Soft bread bruschetta with dried tomatoes and capers accompanied by some vegetables (carrots, celery, courgettes and yellow peppers) with soybean sprouts: all anti-oxidising ingredients. Many coeliacs, once they have had the disease fully diagnosed, are able to radically change their approach to food and in the end, find it completely natural to balance their meals so that all the essential nutrients are accounted for. This also means that your calorie intake is kept under control and in no time at all you'll have a figure that others will envy.

FRIDAY
BREAKFAST – 7.30
Fresh seasonal fruit, a slice of millet bread, a teaspoonful of honey and two walnuts for a breakfast that is rich in sugars, unsaturated fats and fibre and will be more than enough to take you to lunch should you have to miss your morning break.

BREAK – 10.00
Mixed berries (7 oz. / 200 gram mix of strawberries, blackcurrants, blueberries, raspberries) and maybe a piece of dark chocolate to finish off.

LUNCH – 12.30
For lunch, shrimp tempura. This dish is of Japanese origin (and Portuguese before that) and is prepared with fish, shellfish and vegetables that are dipped into a light batter made using iced sparkling water and alternative flours (corn starch, rice flour or similar) and then fried in hot oil with no contamination from flours containing gluten. Some fresh lettuce would be the perfect side dish.

SNACK – 16.30

The mixed berries remaining from your mid-morning break and the last piece of dark chocolate.

DINNER – 20.30

Boiled rice cake with vegetables (tomatoes, spinach, peas and shallots) and, to follow, an omelette roll stuffed with vegetables (courgettes, carrots and so on): a really healthy and delicious dinner prepared with ingredients that are rich in vitamins and anti-oxidants. Over time, many coeliacs learn to cook gluten-free style with great skill and excellent results. They frequently involve friends and relatives in the enthusiasm for "their cooking" and often manage to convert them eating these products, this allowing them to discover spaghetti, biscuits, pastries and unusual breadsticks made from rice and corn or even gluten-free flours that they can use instead of their normal counterparts. Although not necessary, many non- coeliacs get used to this type of cooking and enjoy significant benefits: their meals are more regular for example and they eat less but better.

SATURDAY
BREAKFAST – 8.30

If you usually go jogging early, when you get home don't forget to drink at least 1 litre of water to make sure you are properly hydrated. We'd also suggest a little season fruit to top up your vitamin and salt levels. A nice healthy breakfast would be a few doughnutsmade with gluten-free flour.

LUNCH – 12.30

Tagliatelle with sausages and cocoa: a single dish that will give you energy and a lift. This dish contains starches, proteins, fats, iron, calcium, potassium and sodium. If you are coeliac but don't suffer from high blood pressure, then there's no reason why you can't enjoy a delicious lunch like this but you must always bear in mind that to keep your diet in balance with your needs and maintain varied, balanced and satisfying meals.

SNACK – 16.30

A couple of slices of millet bread with walnuts. If included in your diet, this fantastic cereal will help keep your hair shining and healthy. Walnuts are proving to be one of the healthiest foods that not just coeliacs should learn to appreciate: the fatty acids in walnuts appear to be ideally suited to keeping all types of body tissue young and healthy.

DINNER – 20.30

It's Saturday night and we can allow ourselves a special dinner. Make a promising start with goat's milk cheese and black olive pie accompanied by fresh Sardinian tomini and a sprinkling of aromatic herbs including oregano and thyme. Follow this with *ratatouille* made from aubergines, tomatoes, sweet peppers, celery, black olives and a little garlic. Have rice lasagne with pesto and then bite-sized pieces of chicken with sesame and corn as your second course. Before the coffee, a couple of slices of "salami" made with dark chocolate, brown sugar, eggs, a little butter and a few teaspoonfuls of rum.

SUNDAY
BREAKFAST – 9.00
A cup of partially skimmed cow's milk with rice biscuits and a little natural yoghurt with a few teaspoonfuls of honey.

LUNCH – 13.00
After last night's rich dinner, something very light for lunch would seem appropriate, perhaps a citrus fruit salad (with lemon and orange) enriched with raisins and a little whole plain yoghurt and buckwheat.

SNACK – 16.30
If you're feeling hungry maybe a few sesame seed pastries with some assorted seeds.

DINNER – 20.30
A single dish would be best for dinner. Seeing that it's Sunday, you can allow yourself a nice steak but first make sure that it has all the characteristics that make it healthy. It is always best to choose meat that comes from a large farm where they follow modern naturopathy practices. It may cost a little more than meat from farms where intensive farming is the norm but is well worth the extra as regards the wonderful flavor and for the peace of mind you have from knowing it's healthy food. So, you can enjoy an excellent dinner that will more than satisfy your palate, will not overburden your stomach and at the same time will be easy to digest. After all, tomorrow morning you're back to work so it's better to opt for a meal that doesn't ask too much of you.

A FEW IDEAS FOR EATING OUT
When you are eating out, you need to be very careful not just about the characteristics of what you are being served but also pay attention to what alcoholic drinks contain. Beer is prohibited though nowadays there are *gluten-free* drinks that are permitted and you can always drink wine and spumante. As regards spirits, you will have to live without derivatives of malt and grain (malt whisky or aromatised grappas, myrtle-based spirits, limoncello, rosolio liqueurs, home made or local liqueurs of uncertain provenance, gin, vodka and others) and have at most a small glass of grappa or cognac. According to several studies, straight vodka and whisky are permitted as long as there are no added aromatisers but it's better not to run the risk. When eating in restaurants, it is essential to pick places that cater for coeliacs where the staff understand perfectly what is involved and it is also vital that the pots and pans they use for preparing meals for coeliacs are used for gluten-free cooking only.

IS COELIAC DISEASE A BIND? YES AND NO. THE INGREDIENTS CHANGE, BUT AROMA, FLAVOR, TEXTURE AND TASTE ARE NOT UNATTAINABLE GOALS. THE RESULT? UNUSUALLY FLAVORED BAKED GOODS IN WHICH HEALTH AND PALATE FIND A COMMON GROUND!

How often have we strolled by a bakery and felt immeasurably sad at the thought of all those soft, fragrant products incontrovertibly beyond our reach? This poison slowly but surely eats into our soul, with devious consequences that are even more dangerous for our wellbeing than coeliac disease itself!

Freshly baked bread is difficult to resist, as is the enveloping perfume that is released in the kitchen by delicious breadsticks, pastries and sandwiches. Bakeries are a living nightmare when digestion is a utopia and discomfort our daily companion. Is our beloved bread, one of the cornerstones of the human diet, an unattainable dream, or can we afford to indulge in it once in a while? Nowadays, many shops and supermarkets sell products for coeliacs and those sensitive to gluten. It is possible to prepare or buy bread products that are no way inferior to conventional ones, loaves that are ready made or to be cooked at home, sliced and toasted, and even stored for a week or so. Let's not forget that it is still fairly hard to find gluten-free bread. However, we can prepare it at home and store it for up to ten days, subject to a few precautions, such as storing it in the refrigerator at all times, in a bag, and cutting it only at the last moment. If already sliced, it is best to toast it before storing it away.

But how can we turn home made bread into something tasty reminiscent of the flavors we love? Gluten-free bread has different basic ingredients, and must avoid cereal-based flours such as wheat, kamut, spelt, barley, oats and

BAKED GOODS

rye. Coeliacs and those sensitive to gluten can eat – either in grains or in the form of flour – products such as millet, rice (white, whole, red, Venus, wild), corn, buckwheat, potato starch, cornflour, chickpeas and chestnuts. This rather long list of ingredients can be used to prepare deliciously tasty and textured dishes that are easy to digest. It is possible to find ready blends of flour and yeast suitable to make soft and appetizing baked goods. Or if we prefer, we can mix flours of our own choice, to prepare crumbly loaves made with millet and yoghurt, buckwheat and flax seeds, cornmeal and cheese, and so on. With a bit of experience and initiative, we can create magnificent combinations, resulting in unconventional but by no means inferior breads in terms of flavor and calorie content, adjusted according to our very own needs!

RICOTTA BREADSTICKS

Beer's yeast is used to make beer, bread and pasta. It is a safe ingredient for coeliacs as it is gluten-free. It contains amino acids and biotin (useful in case of dermatitis), and is very rich in B vitamins and minerals such as potassium, magnesium, zinc and phosphorus.

4 servings
Preparation time: **25 minutes**
Cooking time: **15-20 minutes**
Calories per serving: **160**

3/4 cup (100 g) rice flour
1/3 cup (50 g) potato starch
1/3 cup (50 g) cornmeal
1 egg
1 3/4 oz. (50 g) ricotta
1/4 oz. (10 g) beer's yeast
Salt

1. Preheat the oven to 400° F (200° C) and line a baking sheet with greaseproof paper. Sift the flours in a bowl, dissolve the yeast in half a glass of warm, then add the egg and mix together until well combined.

2. Add ricotta, salt to taste and stir together, then knead gently: roll the dough against the sides of the bowl until smooth and holds together. You may need to add a few more tablespoons of water to soften it.

3. Shape the dough into small breadsticks. Work it gently as this type of mixture comes apart easily. The length of the sticks will depend on the baking sheet you're using. Continue with all the remaining dough.

4. Transfer the breadsticks on your baking sheet, keeping them a few inches apart so they won't stick together during cooking.

5. Bake for 15 to 20 minutes or until golden brown. Remove from oven and let cool completely before serving.

CORN BREADSTICKS

Corn is a gluten-free cereal and therefore a safe food for coeliacs. Native to Latin America, where it has been known since 3000 AD, it spread quickly in the Islamic lands of Turkey and from there to all of Europe. It is no accident that Italians call it "granoturco", which is Italian for Turkish corn. It contains a number of minerals, including iron, phosphorus and potassium. It is rich in A and B vitamins, and also antioxidants like zeaxanthin, that has useful anti-ageing properties.

HIGH

4 servings
Preparation time: **25 minutes**
Cooking time: **20 minutes**
Calories per serving: **200**

1/3 cup (40 g) rice flour
1 cup (160 g) cornmeal
1 tbsp xanthan gum
1/8 oz. (5 g) beer's yeast
2 tbsp extra virgin olive oil
Whole salt

1. Preheat the oven to 400° F (200° C) and line a baking sheet with greaseproof paper. Sift the flours in a bowl. Dissolve the xanthan gum in two tablespoons of water, then do the same with the yeast in a separate bowl. Add both liquids to the dry ingredients, and salt to taste.

2. Mix all ingredients together but do not knead. Instead, roll the dough against the sides of the bowl until smooth and holds together. You may need to add a few more tablespoons of water to soften it.

3. Shape the dough into a ball and wrap it in plastic. Let it rest out of the fridge for 30 minutes.

4. Now unwrap the dough and shape your sticks: oil your hands and gently work the dough into thin sticks. Their length will depend on the baking sheet you're using.

5. Transfer the sticks on your sheet one by one, a few inches apart to avoid them from sticking together during cooking.

6. Bake for 20 minutes or until golden brown, then remove from the oven and let cool completely before serving.

SPICED POTATO AND PAPRIKA BREADSTICKS

Potatoes are rich in starch, or long chain sugars, some of which are so resistant to digestive enzymes that they remain intact until evacuation, and therefore have similar physiological effects to dietary fibres. This tuber is also an important source of B and C vitamins, of carotenoids and of polyphenols. Potatoes also contain minerals like iron, zinc and magnesium.

4 servings
Preparation time: **30 minutes**
Cooking time: **20 minutes**
Calories per serving: **180**

1 1/2 lb. (700 g) boiled potatoes
1/3 cup (50 g) rice flour
1/3 cup (50 g) potato starch
1 egg
1 tbsp paprika
1 tbsp spices (pepper, nutmeg, cumin, coriander)
3-4 tbsp olive oil
Salt

1. Preheat the oven to 400° F (200° C) and line a baking sheet with greaseproof paper. Mash the potatoes with a potato masher.

2. Transfer potatoes, starch, rice flour, egg and a pinch of salt onto a handy work surface and mix together without kneading. You may need to oil your hands to prevent the mixture from sticking, so keep oil at hand.

3. Divide the dough into small portions and gently shape them into sticks, about 1/2 inch (1 cm) thick and the length of your baking sheet.

4. Pour the paprika on a plate and the rest of the spices on a separate plate. Roll the sticks in the plate with paprika first, and then in the plate with spices before transferring them onto your baking sheet, a few inches apart so they don't stick together during cooking.

5. Bake for 20 minutes: they'll give off a delicious smell when fully cooked. Once ready, remove from oven and let cool completely before serving.

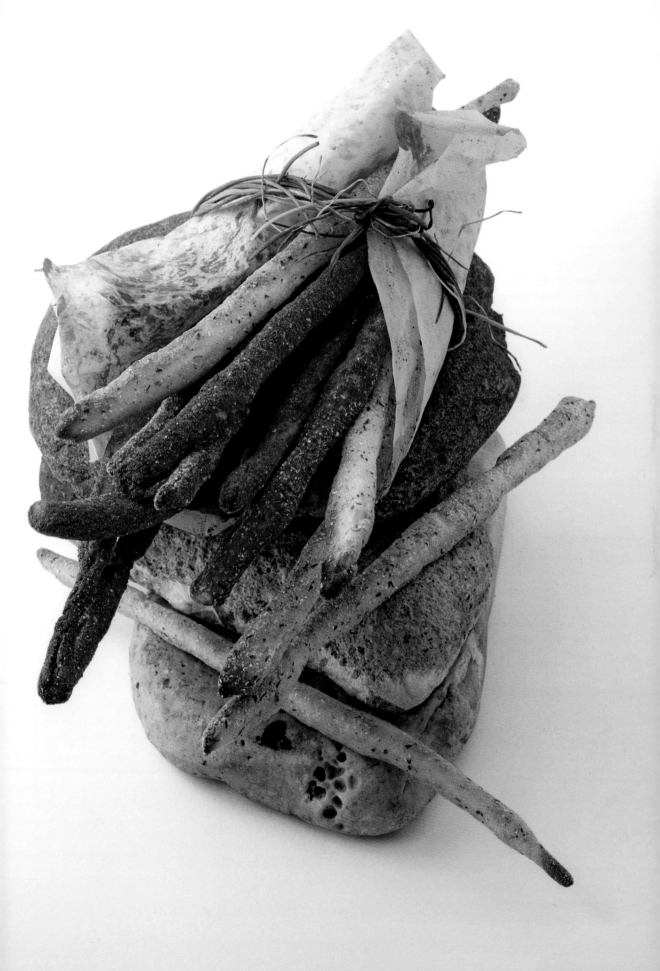

CRISP FLATBREADS WITH PAPRIKA, SESAME AND PUMPKIN SEEDS

Hazelnuts contain unsaturated fatty acids such as omega-3, omega-6, vitamins (A, E and B-complex), and minerals. They are also very rich in calcium. Hazelnut oil is the perfect antioxidant and a good ally against cholesterol: it can help reduce the so called "bad" cholesterol, or LDL.

4 servings
Preparation time: **30 minutes**
Cooking time: **10 minutes**
Calories per serving: **320**

1/3 cup (50 g) rice flour
1/3 cup (50 g) cornmeal
1/3 cup (50 g) potato starch
1/3 cup (50 g) tapioca
1 egg
1 tbsp xanthan gum
2 tbsp (20 g) sesame seeds
2 tbsp (20 g) pumpkin seeds
1 tsp (5 g) paprika
2 tbsp hazelnut oil
Olive oil

1. Preheat the oven to 400° F (200° C) and line a baking sheet with greaseproof paper.

2. In a bowl pour the flours, hazelnut oil and the egg. Dissolve the xanthan gum in two tablespoons of water and then stir into the dry ingredients.

3. Oil your hands with olive oil and knead the dough until smooth. You may need to use some more tablespoons of water to soften it. When the dough holds together and it is free of lumps, transfer it onto a floured work surface and roll it wafer-thin sheet (2 mm). If it cracks, lift it up and shape it into a ball, then press down again and resume rolling.

4. Use a pastry ring to cut your dough into small discs. Pour the sesame, pumpkin seeds and paprika onto three large separate plates. Divide your pastry discs into three groups then roll them into the three different plates with the seeds and spice.

5. Transfer the discs onto your baking sheet and bake for 10 minutes or until golden brown.

6. Remove from oven and let cool completely before serving.

BLACK SESAME SEED CANNOLI

Black sesame seeds are made up of 50% unsaturated fats such as oleic and linoleic acids, that have effective antioxidant properties. They are rich in calcium, phosphorus, selenium, potassium, copper and magnesium. They contain several types of amino acids and A and B vitamins, helping you to regain strength, and are particularly suitable in baby food.

MEDIUM

4 servings
Preparation time: **30 minutes**
Cooking time: **10-15 minutes**
Calories per serving: **235**

1/3 cup (50 g) rice flour
1/ cup (50 g) cornmeal
1/3 cup (50 g) potato starch
1/3 cup. (50 g) corn flour
1 egg
1 tbsp xanthan gum
1/4 oz. (10 g) beer's yeast
2-3 tbsp extra virgin olive oil
2 tbsp (20 g) sesame seeds

1. Preheat the oven to 400° F (200° C) and line a baking sheet with greaseproof paper. Sift the flours in a bowl, add the egg and dissolve the gum in two tablespoons of water, then stir into the flours. Dissolve the yeast in half a glass of warm water, then add to the mixture.

2. Oil your hands and combine all ingredients until you form a smooth dough, then transfer it onto a handy work surface and roll it wafer-thin sheet (1 mm) using a rolling pin. If it cracks, fold it and shape it back into a ball, then press down again and resume rolling.

3. Use a chef's knife to cut 3 inch (8 cm) squares, then wrap them around a cannoli tube, overlap the edges and press them to seal and avoid dough from opening during cooking. Roll your cannoli in a plate full of black sesame seeds.

4. Place them on a baking sheet and bake for 10 to 15 minutes or until golden brown and slightly risen.

5. Remove from oven and let cool completely, then remove the tube. Place in a basket and serve.

CORN BUNS

Corn starch, or corn flour, is a white flour obtained by a particular corn processing method. It is a safe ingredient for coeliacs as it is gluten-free. Corn flour is an ideal thickening agent and has the same properties as corn.

4 servings
Preparation time: **30 minutes**
Cooking time: **15-20 minutes**
Calories per serving: **240**

1 cup (150 g) cornmeal
1/3 cup (50 g) corn flour
1/2 cup (100 ml) yoghurt
1 3/4 oz. (50 g) toma cheese, cubed
1 tbsp baking soda
3-4 tbsp extra virgin olive oil

1. Preheat the oven to 400° F (200° C) and butter a muffin pan or use silicone muffin cups.

2. In a bowl, sift the flours and stir until well combined. In a separate bowl, blend the yoghurt with the baking soda. When the mixture starts to rise, fold the yoghurt into the dry ingredients and mix until well blended.

3. Oil your hands and scoop out a little dough, then knead and shape it into small balls. Add a cube of cheese to every ball and proceed with all the remaining dough.

4. Place the balls in the muffin pan or muffin cups and bake for 15 to 20 minutes. When the buns are ready, your kitchen will be filled with a delicious smell of warm bread. Take the buns out of the oven and let cool completely, then remove them from the pan and serve.

PAN BISCOTTO CHEESE BREAD

Baking soda is derived from mineral deposits of sodium-rich waters and from the ashes of some algae and plants. It has many different uses: in the kitchen it is often used as a raising agent and it's ideal combined with yoghurt.

4 servings
Preparation time: **30 minutes**
Cooking time: **30 minutes**
Calories per serving: **290**

1. Preheat the oven to 350° F (180° C) and line a loaf pan with greaseproof paper. To ease this process, first soak the paper in cold water, then squeeze out excess liquid and finally line the pan.

2. Sift the flours in a large bowl then add the eggs and Pecorino cheese. Mix until well combined.

3. Pour the yoghurt and baking soda into a bowl. Stir the mixture and fold in the dry ingredients as soon as it starts to rise. Knead the dough until smooth..

4. Transfer into the loaf pan.

5. Bake for 30 minutes. Once cooked through, take out of the oven and let cool completely, then remove from pan, discard the greaseproof paper, slice and serve.

1 cup (150 g) cornmeal
1/3 cup (50 g) corn flour
1 tbsp baking soda
1/2 cup (100 ml) yoghurt
2 eggs
1/3 cup (50 g) freshly grated
Pecorino cheese

MILLET BREAD WITH WALNUTS

Flaxseed oil is made up of almost 90% unsaturated fatty acids. It contains lecithin, that helps the proper functioning of our nervous system, and vitamin E, which is rich in antioxidants, helps skin heal faster, and counteracts cardiovascular diseases. Once opened, keep refrigerated as it is perishable and deteriorates easily.

4 servings
Preparation time: **30 minutes**
Cooking time: **40 minutes**
Calories per serving: **380**

11/2 cup (200 g) millet flour
1/3 cup (50 g) potato starch
11/4 cup (300 ml) yoghurt
1 tsp baking soda
3/4 oz. (20 g) walnuts
2 tbsp flaxseed oil

1. Preheat the oven to 350° F (180° C) and line a loaf pan with greaseproof paper. To ease this process, first soak the paper in cold water, then squeeze out the excess liquid and line the pan.

2. In a bowl, sift the flours and stir well. Mix the yoghurt and baking soda in a different bowl. When the mixture starts to rise, incorporate the liquid batter into the flour mixture. Add the flaxseed oil and keep stirring until the dough is smooth and holds together well.

3. Place the loaf in the pan and sprinkle with walnuts, pressing well with your fingers to incorporate them into the dough.

4. Bake for 40 minutes, then remove from the oven and sprinkle the crust with a few tablespoons of cold water. Cover the pan so that the crust doesn't turn too hard and crumbly. Leave to cool, then remove from the pan, discard the greaseproof paper, slice and serve.

BUCKWHEAT FLOUR BREAD

Buckwheat is a gluten-free broadleaf plant native to Asia. The seeds are triangular in shape and deteriorate quickly when exposed to the air. Buckwheat flour is the main ingredient in two traditional Northern Italian foods: polenta taragna and pizzoccheri. It contains essential amino acids that cannot be synthesized by the body, and also calcium, phosphorus, potassium, magnesium, zinc, manganese, iron, vitamin E and B-complex vitamins. It is also rich in rutin (which aids blood vessel health) and in chiro-inositol, boasting supposed anti-diabetic properties.
.

MEDIUM

4 servings
Preparation time: **30 minutes**
Resting time: **30 minutes**
Cooking time: **30 minutes**
Calories per serving: **320**

1. Preheat the oven to 350° F (180° C) and line a baking sheet with greaseproof paper.

2. Sift the flours into a bowl, add the flaxseed oil and mix well. Place the yeast and water in a separate bowl, and mix together. Pour the liquid into the dry ingredients and mix. Cover the dough and let it rise in a warm place for 30 minutes.

3. Shape the dough into small balls. You may need to oil your hands to prevent the mixture from sticking. Place the buns on the greaseproof paper-lined baking sheet a few inches apart, so they won't stick together. Sprinkle the small loaves with flax seeds and place in the oven to cook.

4. Bake for 30 minutes, remove from oven and leave to cool before serving.

11/4 cup (150 g) buckwheat flour
1/3 cup (50 g) potato starch
1/4 oz. (10 g) beer's yeast
1/2 cup (100 ml) water
4 tsp flaxseed oil
3 tbsp (30 g) flax seeds

CHESTNUT FLOUR BREAD

Sunflower seeds have the lowest calorie content among oily seeds. They are made up of about 45% fats, between 20% and 28% proteins, and about 23% carbohydrates. They are very rich in A, D, E and B-complex vitamins and they also contain minerals like magnesium, iron, zinc, copper, manganese and cobalt, as well as chlorogenic, linoleic and folic acids.

MEDIUM

4 servings
Preparation time: **30 minutes**
Cooking time: **40 minutes**
Calories per serving: **380**

1 cup. (150 g) chestnut flour
3/4 cup (100 g) potato starch
1/4 cup (50 ml) warm water
1/2 cup (100 ml) yoghurt
1 tbsp baking soda
2 tbsp (20 g) sunflower seeds
2 tbsp (20 g) pumpkin seeds

1. Preheat the oven to 350° F (180° C) and line a loaf pan with greaseproof paper. To ease this process, first soak the paper in cold water, then squeeze out the excess liquid and line the pan.

2. In a bowl, sift the flours, add the water and seeds, then stir to mix. Should the mixture require more water, add half a glass, pouring a little at a time.

3. In a separate bowl, mix the yoghurt with the baking soda. When it starts to rise, quickly stir in the dry ingredients and work the mixture until smooth and free of lumps, then transfer it into the pan and put it in the oven.

4. Bake the loaf for about 30 minutes. Once cooked through, remove the pan from oven and let cool completely; then remove the loaf from the pan, remove the paper, slice and serve.

RICE FLOUR AND SESAME BREAD

Potato starch is starch extracted from potatoes and other tubers. It is gluten-free and therefore used to replace wheat flour. It is often used in coeliac-friendly recipes to soften the dough and help the ingredients hold together.

4 servings
Preparation time: **30 minutes**
Resting time: **80 minutes**
Cooking time: **40 minutes**
Calories per serving: **380**

1 cup (150 g) rice flour
4 tbsp (30 g) potato starch
1/3 cup (50 g) cornmeal
5 tbsp (30 g) carob flour
1/4 oz. (10 g) beer's yeast
1 cup (250 ml) warm water
4 tbsp extra virgin olive oil
1 tbsp (10 g) sesame seeds

1. Preheat the oven to 350° F (180° C) and line a rectangular baking tin with greaseproof paper.

2. Dissolve the yeast in half a glass of warm water. Sift the flours into a bowl, then add the oil, yeast and remaining water. Knead the dough until smooth and elastic.

3. Cover the dough and let rise for 30 minutes in a warm place. Place it in the tin, cover with a damp dish cloth, and let rise for a further 50 minutes.

4. When the dough is ready, brush the upper surface with water and then sprinkle it with sesame seeds.

5. Bake it for about 40 minutes or until golden brown. When the loaf is cooked through, remove the tin from the oven and let it cool completely, then slice the bread and serve.

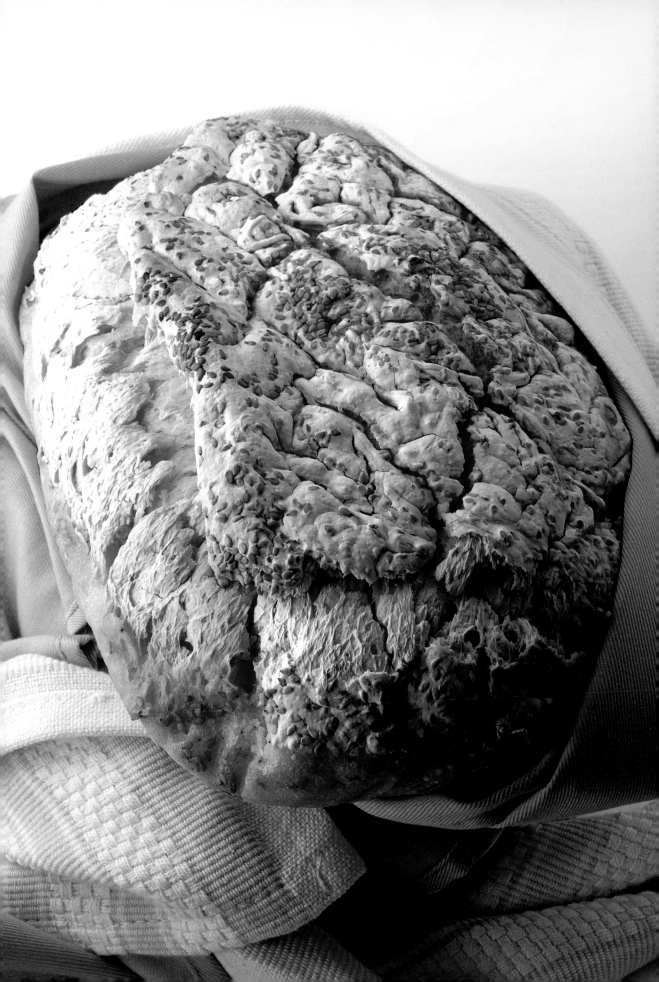

COELIACS OFTEN HAVE TO GIVE UP ON CERTAIN PLEASURES OF THE PALATE, AND EXERCISE PARTICULAR CAUTION WHEN THEY ARE NOT CERTAIN ABOUT THE ORIGIN OF THEIR FOOD. HERE ARE A FEW STARTERS THAT ARE TASTY, EASY TO PREPARE, AND ABOVE ALL, SAFE.

At a first glance, coeliac disease could be likened to a prison sentence without the chance of appeal, with bread, breadsticks, crackers, sandwiches, and even biscuits being totally out of bounds! And yet, safe alternatives do exit: we just need to know where to look for them. Let's imagine we are at the grocery store. What can we put in our shopping cart, and what should we avoid at all costs?

Beware of cold cuts, cheese spreads, compotes, sauces, and so on: we rarely read the labels, and therefore mistakenly think that these foods do not contain wheat. And yet, as this cereal is an effective thickener, it can easily be found in these and other foods, for example ham and salami. It is always best to err on the side of caution, and make absolutely sure that such products do not contain gluten or wheat by carefully reading the list of ingredients. However, things change if we decide to avoid pre-packaged foods, and start preparing our meals at home (unfortunately, the problem is unavoidable when we eat out, as it can be hard to find appropriate solutions outside the home). Supermarkets are gearing up to offer valid alternatives, and not just with regard to pre-packed foods and ready meals. And so, we can fill our cart with rice, buckwheat and corn rice, or with potato starch and cornmeal. We might wonder why coeliac disease and gluten intolerance are on the up, but we must consider that our diet, from breakfast through to dinner, is often unbalanced, making excessive use of wheat flour, which is present in more than two-thirds of what we eat. Therefore it makes sense to replace part of it with other cereals.

We have tried to put ourselves in the shoes of those suffering from coeliac disease, so

STARTERS

■ ■ ■ ■ ■ ■ ■

as to understand the choices they need to make day after day in order to stay healthy. In devising our recipes, we have focused on the various meals of the day, and on the sacrifices, big and small, that coeliacs are forced to make. The result is a series of simple dishes suited to everyday. For our starters, we have created dishes based on ingredients that can be bought ready-made. Delicious corn nachos, for example, dipped in a simple tomato sauce, can be transformed into a quick and easy appetiser or starter. And then there are tasty bruschettas, made using a mixture of flours specially planned for those who need or want to replace flours containing gluten with those based on grasses. These products can be found in shops selling organic produce or in supermarkets selling alternative foods. Using these flours in the right amounts, following the doses provided in these recipes or developing your own as you gain experience, you can indulge in no end of focaccias, crostinis and pancakes.

RICE BREAD BRUSCHETTA

Due to their content of vitamins A and E, lycopenes, and beta-carotene, tomatoes are excellent antioxidants. All of these substances are well known for their ability to prevent cancer and degenerative diseases. Furthermore, they help the heart and blood circulation, as well as improving eyesight.

MEDIUM

4 servings
Preparation time: **25 minutes**
Cooking time: **30 minutes**
Calories per serving: **250**

For the dough:
1 1/4 cup (200 g) rice flour
1/3 cup (50 g) potato starch
1 egg
3 tbsp extra virgin olive oil
1/2 cup (100 ml) yoghurt
1 tsp baking soda

For the sauce:
14 oz. (400 g) plum tomatoes, ripe
1 clove of garlic
1 bunch basil
4 tbsp extra virgin olive oil
Salt
Pepper

1. Preheat the oven to 350° F (180° C). On a wooden pastry board, make a well in the centre of the flours, then break the egg into it and add two tablespoons of olive oil and half a glass of water. Knead with your hands for at least 10 minutes, until the dough is smooth and free of lumps.

2. Mix the yoghurt and baking soda in a bowl. When the mixture starts to rise, fold in the flours and knead until all the ingredients have blended together. Oil your hands from time to time to keep the dough from sticking, then scoop out some dough and shape it into buns.

3. Quickly arrange the buns on a baking sheetlined with greaseproof paper and bake for about 30 minutes.

4. Meanwhile, clean, wash and dice the tomatoes. Sieve the excess liquid. Peel the garlic and chop it into small pieces. Clean, wash and mince the basil. Put the tomatoes, garlic and basil in a bowl. Add four tablespoons of oil, season with salt and pepper to taste, then stir.

5. When ready, remove the bread from the oven and let it cool slightly. Serve the tomato mixture on the slices of bread or alongside them.

CORN BRUSCHETTA
WITH SUN-DRIED TOMATOES AND CAPERS

Capers are the flower buds of the Capparis spinosa, a perennial shrub. They are a good source of proteins, vitamins A, E, K and of the B-complex, and minerals such as iron, copper, manganese and magnesium. As they are often preserved in salt, it is important to soak them in water, rinsing them repeatedly. They stimulate the appetite, aid digestion, help reduce fluid retention and have diuretic properties.

MEDIUM

4 servings
Preparation time: **40 minutes**
Cooking time: **35 minutes**
Calories per serving: **350**

For the bread:
1 cup (150 g) cornmeal
1/3 cup (50 g) corn flour
1/2 cup (100 ml) yoghurt
1 tbsp baking soda
2 eggs
1/3 cup (50 g) grated Pecorino cheese

For the sauce:
8 sun-dried tomatoes
3/4 oz. (20 g) capers preserved in salt
1 clove of garlic
1 sprig parsley
1 yellow bell pepper
2 tbsp extra virgin olive oil
Salt

1. Preheat the oven to 350° F (180° C) and line a loaf pan with greaseproof paper. In order to make the paper stick to the pan, soak it in cold water, squeeze out the excess liquid and then line the pan.

2. In a bowl, sift the flours, add the eggs and about half a glass of water, then add the Pecorino cheese. Mix the ingredients until they combine.

3. Mix the yoghurt and baking soda in a bowl. When the mixture starts to rise, fold in the flour mixture and knead until all the ingredients have blended together.

4. Pour the batter into the pan and bake for about 30 minutes. When the bread is ready, remove it from the oven and let it cool completely before turning it out of the pan.

5. Clean, wash and chop the parsley, keeping some sprigs aside as garnish. Peel and mince the garlic. Wash the pepper, remove the stem, seeds and white parts, then cut it into thin strips.

6. In a hot non-stick pan, toast the garlic, capers, pepper and minced parsley on high heat for a few minutes. Stir regularly to keep from burning.

7. Soak the tomatoes in a bowl of warm water for 5 minutes, then drain and add them to the other ingredients, seasoning with salt to taste and drizzling the oil. Slice the bread and arrange the slices on a serving dish. Spread the caper mixture on each slice, and garnish with freshly minced parsley.

CORN CHIPS WITH SPICY TOMATO SAUCE

Coriander is a grassy plant native to the Mediterranean, appreciated above all, in a culinary context, for the distinctive spicy flavor of its leaves. It has considerable digestive properties, effectively fighting stomach cramps and bloating. It is also an excellent stimulant due to the presence of anti-fatigue, bacteriostatic and fungicidal substances.

4 servings
Preparation time: **10 minutes**
Cooking time: **10 minutes**
Calories per serving: **200**

3 1/2 oz. (100 g) corn nachos
4 ripe tomatoes
1 tbsp paprika
1 jalapeño chilli pepper
1 tbsp (10 g) fresh coriander
1 tbsp extra virgin olive oil
1 tbsp pepper

1. Preheat the oven to 400° F (220° C).

2. Clean, wash and dice the tomatoes. Drain off the excess water in a strainer, and after 5 minutes transfer them into a bowl.

3. Wash and cut the chilli pepper into rings. Clean, wash and mince the coriander. Add the paprika, coriander, chilli, pepper and oil to the tomatoes, then stir.

4. Place the nachos in an oven-proof dish and allow to heat for 10 minutes.

5. Once ready, transfer them into a serving bowl or onto individual dishes. Serve the tomato sauce directly on the nachos or alongside them in small individual bowls.

SMOKED SALMON WITH POTATO STARCH PANCAKES

Salmon contains phosphorus, proteins, iron and calcium. Moreover, it is rich in omega-3 fatty acids, which boost muscle growth - especially useful for sports people - and lower cholesterol. Omega-3 is essential in the prevention of blood vessel diseases and to fight visual impairment in the elderly, especially with regard to the macula of the retina.

MEDIUM

4 servings
Preparation time: **15 minutes**
Cooking time: **7 minutes**
Calories per serving: **320**

For the pancakes:
1 tbsp rice flour
2 tbsp potato starch
2 eggs
1 3/4 cup (400 ml) milk
Oil as needed to grease
the pan
Salt (optional)

For the filling:
6 1/2 oz. (180 g) smoked
salmon, sliced

To garnish:
1 red onion
3/4 oz. (20 g) capers
preserved in brine
1 head of lettuce
Salt
Pepper

1. Clean, wash and dry the lettuce gently, then keep it aside, wrapped in a damp cloth, until ready for use. Peel and slice the onion into rings. Drain off the brine from the capers.

2. Pour the flours, milk and eggs into a bowl and whisk the ingredients using an electric mixer, until the mixture is smooth and free of lumps. If you wish, you can add a pinch of salt.

3. Grease a 10 inch (25 cm) non-stick pan with kitchen paper soaked in oil. Using a ladle, pour some mixture into the hot pan. Cook for a minute and, when the pancakes come away easily from the sides of the pan, flip them over and cook on the other side. Continue until all the mixture is used up, then arrange the pancakes on a plate.

4. Stuff the pancakes with the salmon and close them at will, for example by rolling or folding them. Arrange the salad leaves on a serving dish and place the pancakes on top, garnished with the capers and onion rings. Season with salt and pepper to taste.

RED CABBAGE SPRING ROLLS

Cabbages are very suitable for dieting as they are low in calories. They contain vegetable proteins and a great deal of vitamin C (pound for pound, cabbage has twice the vitamin C content of oranges), as well as B-complex vitamins and vitamins A and K. Furthermore, they are high in minerals such as copper, iron, calcium and phosphorus. Ideal for the treatment of ulcerative colitis and stomach ulcers, they also facilitate the production of red blood cells and counteract forms of anaemia. Moreover, they contain indoles, sulforaphane (a sulphur-based substance, hence its unpleasant smell) and other antioxidants suitable for the prevention of degenerative diseases in the elderly.

MEDIUM

4 servings
Preparation time: **20 minutes**
Cooking time: **4 minutes**
Calories per serving: **220**

8 rice sheets
1 head of baby lettuce
7 oz. (200 g) red cabbage
Rice flour as needed
Sunflower oil as needed
Tamari sauce as needed
Salt
Pepper

1. Clean, wash and dry the baby lettuce and cabbage. Cut them into strips with a knife, keeping them separate and setting aside four whole cabbage leaves as garnish.

2. On a large dish, wet the sheets of rice individually in cold water and let them soften for a minute, then arrange them on a smooth surface and gently pat them to remove any excess water. Stuff them with the salad and cabbage. Season with salt and pepper to taste, then wrap the edge of the sheets inwards to form small rolls.

3. Roll these in flour until fully coated. Heat plenty of oil in a non-stick pan and, when hot, dip in the rolls and fry them for 3-4 minutes, until crispy. When cooked, drain the rolls and place them on a paper towel to remove the excess oil.

4. Arrange the red cabbage leaves on 4 individual dishes and place two rolls on top of each. Serve them with bowls of tamari sauce, to which you can add a few strips of red cabbage. Serve the spring rolls hot.

COURGETTE AND SALMON ROLLS

Courgettes are easy to digest and low in calories, making them ideal for low-calorie diets. They contain 94% water, as well as various minerals such as potassium, iron, calcium and phosphorus. They are rich in vitamins (A, C, B1 and B2), bioflavonoids and antioxidants such as lutein and zeaxanthin, which perform an effective anti-ageing action, fighting some of the ailments typical of old age. They also have significant diuretic, laxative and purifying properties.

MEDIUM

4 servings
Preparation time: **20 minutes**
Cooking time: **10 minutes**
Calories per serving: **220**

2 courgettes
7 oz. (200 g) fresh salmon,
cut into thin slices
1 3/4 oz. (50 g) soy noodles
1 3/4 oz. (50 g) fresh ricotta
Sunflower oil as needed
2 tbsp tamari sauce
Salt
Pepper

1. Cook the noodles for about a minute in a pot with plenty of salted boiling water, then drain in a strainer.

2. Transfer them into a bowl and pour over the tamari, then stir and let cool, enabling the flavor to blend and the noodles to colour slightly. Set them aside until ready for use.

3. Trim, wash and cut the courgettes into long, wafer-thin sheet slices using a mandolin slicer. Cut the salmon into slices roughly the size of the vegetable strips. Overlay the courgette and salmon slices, cover them with some ricotta cheese, then add salt and pepper to taste.

4. Roll up the ingredients and close them by wrapping some of the noodles around them.

5. Heat plenty of oil in a non-stick pan to 340° F (170° C), fry the rolls for 4-5 minutes until nicely browned, then drain. Dry the excess oil by wrapping them in kitchen paper, then transfer them onto a serving platter and serve.

CAPRINO CHEESE AND OLIVE CROSTINI

Olives are made up of 50% water and 15%-35% unsaturated vegetable fats, depending on the type and degree of ripeness. Ash and fibres make up 6%-10% of the total weight. Their fats lower the level of cholesterol in the blood and perform an antioxidant action, also through the presence of phenols. Olives are also a good source of potassium and other minerals, and have digestive and energising properties. Black olives are higher in fat and calories than the green varieties.

 EASY

4 servings
Preparation time: **10 minutes**
Calories per serving: **280**

1. Remove all the hard, woody parts from the herbs and finely chop the leaves with a mincing knife or blender, keeping one third aside as garnish.

2. Drain the olives, cut them in half lengthwise, and remove the pit. Set them aside until ready for use.

3. Pour the cheese into a bowl then work it with a fork until smooth. Add the minced herbs and olive oil, season with salt and pepper to taste, and stir.

4. Spread some cheese mixture onto each bun using a knife. Garnish with a few olive pieces and season with the remaining herbs.

4 rice buns
7 oz. (200 g) fresh goat's cheese
2 oz. (60 g) black olives
1 bunch herbs (oregano and thyme)
1 tbsp extra virgin olive oil
Salt
Pepper

NUT AND APPLE SALAD

Apples are a good source of vitamins C, B1 and B2, as well as minerals such as potassium, magnesium, phosphorus, calcium and sodium. Unlike other fruits, they do not ferment, which means they can be eaten at the end of a meal. Moreover, they contain pectin, a fibre that is very useful for the gastrointestinal system and that contributes to reducing blood sugar levels.

EASY

4 servings
Preparation time: **10 minutes**
Calories per serving: **110**

1. Wash and peel the apple and pear, then cut them into pieces at will. Put them into a bowl and add the nuts. Drain the artichokes of their oil and add them to the other ingredients.

2. Squeeze the lemon juice into a bowl, add the oil, season with salt and pepper to taste, then stir.

3. Clean, wash and dry the two types of salad and arrange them on a plate. Add the fresh fruit and nuts. Season with the lemon sauce, stir and serve.

4. If you wish, you can serve the salad with rice croutons or with crispy wafers made using gluten-free flours.

1 apple
1 pear
3/4 oz. (20 g) almonds, shelled
3/4 oz. (20 g) pistachio nuts, shelled
1/4 oz. (10 g) baby artichokes in oil
1 3/4 oz. (50 g) curly lettuce
1 3/4 oz. (50 g) chicory
1 lemon
2 tbsp extra virgin olive oil
Salt
Pepper

MOZZARELLA AND TOMATO MILLE-FEUILLE

Mozzarella is a typical Mediterranean cheese. It is rich in milk protein (casein), calcium and vitamin D, all substances that actively fight osteoporosis. It is a fresh product that is high in water, and therefore performs a greater purifying action than seasoned cheese. Like all uncooked cheeses, the presence of casein may make it less digestible than cooked, seasoned varieties (such as Parmesan, for example), in which the casein transforms over time.

 EASY

4 servings
Preparation time: **10 minutes**
Calories per serving: **350**

1. Clean, wash and slice the tomatoes. Arrange the slices on a slightly tilted wooden chopping board to remove the excess liquid.

2. Drain the mozzarella and cut it into thin slices. Clean and wash the basil, then dab it dry with a cotton cloth or kitchen paper.

3. Cut the bread into slices: you can use a pastry ring to create special shapes, like circles or triangles.

4. On individual plates, alternate slices of bread, tomato and mozzarella, topping each triple layer with a few basil leaves. When serving, drizzle with a tablespoon of olive oil and season with salt and pepper to taste. Garnish the mille-feuille with the remaining basil, and serve.

7 oz. (200 g) buckwheat flour bread
3 ripe tomatoes
8 3/4 oz. (250 g) mozzarella
1 bunch basil
4 tbsp extra virgin olive oil
Salt
Pepper

NUTTY VEGETARIAN BALLS

Raisins are a variety of dried fruit of which there are several types, most commonly deriving from the "sultana" grape. Raisins have the same properties as fresh grapes, but are higher in calories. They are rich in minerals (potassium, phosphorus, magnesium, calcium and fluorine), vitamins (A, C and B-complex) and various types of tannin, particularly in the peel. As a result, they have a purifying, detoxifying, tonic and mildly laxative effect, as well as effectively fighting high blood pressure, constipation, gout, atherosclerosis and arthritis.

MEDIUM

4 servings
Preparation time: **25 minutes**
Cooking time: **15 minutes**
Calories per serving: **260**

7 oz. (200 g) tofu
1 bell pepper
1 aubergine
3/4 oz. (20 g) raisins, soaked
3/4 oz. (20 g) pine nuts
3/4 oz. (20 g) pistachio nuts
2 tbsp (20 g) light sesame seeds
2 eggs
1/3 cup (50 g) rice flour
1/3 cup (50 g) grated Parmesan cheese
Salt
Pepper

1. Preheat the oven to 400° F (200° C) and line a baking sheet with greaseproof paper.

2. Clean, wash and chop the vegetables into small pieces. Drain the tofu and chop it into small pieces. Let the vegetables and tofu simmer in a non-stick pan for about 5 minutes or until the vegetables have reached the desired consistency. If necessary, spray with a few tablespoons of hot water.

3. In a mortar, finely crush the nuts, then transfer them into a bowl with the vegetables and tofu. Squeeze the raisins dry, then add them to the mixture, with the Parmesan cheese, eggs and sesame seeds. Stir until the mixture is well blended, seasoning with salt and pepper.

4. Take a little of the mixture at a time and roll it into a ball with your hands. Roll each ball in flour to keep them compact while cooking. As you make them, place the balls on the baking sheet, and then bake them for about 10 minutes. Remove them from the oven, transfer them onto a serving dish, and serve.

PEAR AND CHEESE RICE FOCACCIA

Pears are rich in soluble and insoluble fibre. A single pear provides 20% of the daily fibre requirement of an adult, helping to reduce cholesterol and aiding the functioning of the gastro-intestinal tract. By slowing the intake of fructose, these fibres hydrate the body and help keep constant levels of energy while performing strenuous physical work.

MEDIUM

4 servings
Preparation time: **35 minutes**
Resting time: **30 minutes**
Cooking time: **20 minutes**
Calories per serving: **240**

For the dough:
3/4 cup (100 g) rice flour
1/3 cup (50 g) cornmeal
1/3 cup (50 g) corn flour
1/4 oz. (10 g) beer's yeast
1 tbsp xanthan gum
2-4 tbsp extra virgin olive oil
Water as needed

For the filling:
1 pear
1 3/4 oz. (50 g) Gorgonzola cheese
1 3/4 oz. (50 g) mozzarella
Pepper

1. Preheat the oven to 400° F (200° C) and line a baking sheet with greaseproof paper. Place the flour mixture on a wooden pastry board and make a well in the centre. Dissolve the xanthan gum and yeast separately, in half a glass of water each, then pour both liquids into the well. Knead until the mixture is smooth.

2. Oil your hands from time to time to work the ingredients more easily. If necessary, add a few spoonfuls of water to soften the dough, then wrap it in cling film and let it rest for 30 minutes.

3. Wash, dry and slice the pear. Chop the cheeses into small pieces.

4. Roll the dough out onto the baking sheet and add the slices of pear, pressing lightly with your fingers so that they incorporate into the mixture while cooking. Add the diced cheese and bake for around 20 minutes.

5. Once cooked, remove the focaccia from the oven, transfer it onto a serving dish, season with pepper, and serve.

CORN AND SOY PASTA, RICE SPAGHETTI AND POTATO GNOCCHI ARE JUST SOME OF THE ALTERNATIVES AVAILABLE TO COELIACS. FOR THOSE WANTING TO EXPERIMENT, HERE ARE ALL THE SECRETS TO PREPARING TAGLIATELLE, LASAGNE AND OTHER TASTY, HEALTHY FIRST COURSES.

There are many valid first course alternatives on the market, conceived especially for coeliacs and those who suffer from gluten intolerance . It has become very easy to find rice spaghetti, corn penne, soy noodles, and so on. It is more difficult to find more specific products such as tagliatelle, gnocchi, lasagne or pizza. The latter, for example, can be prepared at home with good results by mixing rice flour, cornmeal, brewer's

yeast and a few tablespoons of olive oil. If the dough won't bind, you can always add an egg. Compared to the highly thickening flours containing gluten, those based on grasses, which are gluten free, bind with difficulty, so the most important ingredient is patience! These flours tend to divide, and therefore, rather than kneading them, they need to be combined gently, following their nature and without ever forcing them. It is merely a matter of habit and a small element of skill. You can adopt small tricks, for example using egg, the protein and fat of which are effective thickeners and can combine the flours, enabling you to create doughs and pastries. Ricotta cheese is also a good way to keep ingredients together: gnocchi can be a hard challenge, but by adding this dairy product they become easier to knead, and when cooked, its proteins make them more flexible, so that they will not fall apart so easily.

Xanthan gum (identified on labels as E415) is also a great thickener, especially in recipes where thinness and flexibility are of the essence, such as lasagne and tagliatelle. When preparing healthy meals on a par with wheat-based foods, the most elaborate recipes become a challenge in which to unleash the full power of your cooking skills!

And the goodness of these meals will certainly not suffer: the pizza dough will be

FIRST COURSES

soft and yielding, forming the perfect base for the tomato sauce and cheese. Furthermore, its almost neutral taste will enhance rather than cover the flavor of the other ingredients. Egg tagliatelle, which absorb seasonings well, have a smooth, complete taste: you'll hardly believe that they have been prepared with a mixture of grasses bound with xanthan gum. In dishes where cocoa is the main ingredient, this powder will clearly overpower the other ingredients with his powerful personality. Cocoa powder, on its own, does not have a great thickening power, but, combined with ricotta cheese, it will bind very well with the potatoes of your gnocchi. For the chocolate tagliatelle with xanthan, rest is the most important ingredient: by leaving the dough in the refrigerator for a day, the dough will become more flexible and easier to roll out and cut into strips. The pasta's slightly bitter taste (which can be lessened with a pinch of sugar) is very appetizing when mixed with creams.

CHEESE FARINATA

Chickpeas contain 6% of sugar and fat, but also many proteins, amino acids and fibres. Therefore, they are ideal to keep the digestive system regular. They are rich in vitamins (E, C, K and of the B-complex) and minerals such as potassium, phosphorus, calcium and magnesium. These pulses help reduce LDL cholesterol levels and homocysteine, an amino acid that increases vascular disease. Their heart-protective effect is further increased by their content of of omega-3 fatty acids.

MEDIUM

4 servings
Preparation time: **20 minutes**
Resting time: **1 hour**
Cooking time: **13 minutes**
Calories per serving: **180**

2 cups (200 g) gram flour
2 cups (500 ml) water
1 3/4 oz. (50 g) Gorgonzola cheese
4 tbsp extra virgin olive oil
1 sprig of sage
1 sprig of rosemary
Salt
Pepper

1. Preheat the oven to 480° F (250° C). Slowly pour the gram flour into 2 cups (500 ml) of water, and stir until the mixture is smooth and free of lumps.

2. Season with salt to taste and leave to stand for about an hour. Dice the Gorgonzola cheese and keep aside until ready for use. Wash and dry the sage and rosemary.

3. Oil the bottom and sides of a tart pan (sides must be max. 1 inch/3 cm high). Gently pour the batter into the pan using a wooden spoon and making sure the oil mixes with the farinata, then level the top and bake for about 10 minutes. Once cooked, remove from the oven, add the cheese and bake for a further 3 minutes (or until the Gorgonzola cheese has melted).

4. Remove the pan from the oven, cut into squares and then sprinkle with pepper. Garnish and season with sage leaves and a few sprigs of rosemary. Serve hot.

PIZZA MARGHERITA

Beef tomatoes contain 94% water, making them purifying and refreshing. Due to their content of vitamins A and E, lycopenes and beta-carotene, these tomatoes are excellent antioxidants. All of these substances are well known for their ability to prevent cancer and degenerative diseases. They help blood circulation and the proper functioning of the heart, and have protective effects on the eyesight.

MEDIUM

4 servings
Preparation time: **30 minutes**
Resting time: **30 minutes**
Cooking time: **30 minutes**
Calories per serving: **270**

For the dough:
3/4 cup (100 g) rice flour
1/3 cup (50 g) cornmeal
1/3 cup (50 g) corn flour
1/4 oz. (10 g) beer's yeast
1 tbsp xanthan gum
2 tbsp extra virgin olive oil
Water as needed

For the filling:
7 oz. (200 g) mozzarella
4 ripe beef tomatoes
4 sprigs thyme
2 tbsp oil
Salt

1. Preheat the oven to 400° F (200° C) and line a 12 inch (30 cm) baking pan with greaseproof paper. Strip half of the thyme leaves from the stem and keep the rest whole as garnish.

2. On a wooden pastry board, make a well in the flour mixture. Dissolve the xanthan gum and yeast separately, in two tablespoons of water each, then pour both liquids in the centre of the well. Add the oil and knead the ingredients until smooth and firm. Spray with a few tablespoons of water if needed. Wrap the dough in cling film and leave to rest for 30 minutes.

3. Wash, slice, seed and peel the tomatoes, keeping the fillets. Drain the excess water in a sieve for 5 minutes. Strain the mozzarella and dice.

4. Roll out the dough on the baking sheet. Sprinkle it with sliced tomatoes and diced mozzarella, then season with olive oil and thyme leaves. Add salt to taste. Cook the pizza for about 30 minutes, then remove it from the oven. Garnish with the remaining thyme, and serve.

RICOTTA GNOCCHI WITH BLUE CHEESE AND PUMPKIN

Pumpkin is a low-calorie food with many nutritional properties. It contains minerals such as calcium, iron, potassium and phosphorus, It is also rich in fibre, B-complex vitamins, and vitamins A and C. It has soothing, digestive and refreshing properties, and is useful to keep the digestive system regular and to cleanse the kidneys. It is the perfect choice for low-calorie diets.

HIGH

4 servings
Preparation time: **50-60 minutes**
Cooking time: **15 minutes**
Calories per serving: **400**

For the gnocchi:
1 1/3 lbs. (600 g) potatoes, boiled and peeled
3/4 cup (100 g) corn flour
1 egg
3 1/2 oz. (100 g) fresh ricotta
Rice flour
Salt

For the sauce:
14 oz. (400 g) pumpkin
2 1/2 oz. (70 g) blue cheese
1 3/4 oz. (50 g) butter
2 sprigs of sage
Salt
Pepper

1. Arrange the flour, ricotta, mashed potatoes (mashed with a potato masher) and egg on a wooden pastry board. Add a little salt and combine the ingredients without kneading, as this is a fragile dough that falls apart easily.

2. When the mixture is firm, cut it into pieces a little at a time. Roll out the pieces of dough on a work surface and shape them into logs of about 1/3 x 4 inches (1 x 10 cm). Chop them into small pieces and shape the gnocchi by pressing lightly with a fork. Repeat until all the mixture is used up. Arrange the gnocchi on a kitchen towel sprinkled with rice flour so that they do not stick together.

3. Gently wash and dry the sage. Cut the pumpkin into pieces, discarding the rind, seeds and stringy parts. Stew the pumpkin in a non-stick pan, to the desired consistency (approx. 10 minutes). Once cooked, transfer it into a soup tureen, large enough to hold the gnocchi once ready.

4. Dice the butter and the blue cheese and combine with the pumpkin in the soup tureen. Bring a pot filled with plenty of salted water to the boil. Toss the gnocchi into the pot and cook until they float. Fish them out with a skimmer and transfer them into the soup tureen, then stir gently to bind the ingredients together. Add salt and pepper to taste, garnish with sage leaves and serve.

COCOA GNOCCHI
WITH CREAM AND POMEGRANATE

Cocoa contains minerals such as magnesium, potassium, calcium, phosphorus, iron and sodium. It is high in stimulants such as caffeine, tyramine, serotonin and phenylethylamine (which are suitable to produce endorphins), and contains vitamins of the B-complex. Cocoa has anti-inflammatory, antioxidant and anti-migraine properties, but, above all, it is stimulating and energising.

4 servings
Preparation time: **50-60 minutes**
Cooking time: **10 minutes**
Calories per serving: **360**

For the gnocchi:
1 1/3 lbs. (600 g) potatoes, boiled and peeled
3/4 cup (100 g) corn flour
1 egg
3 1/2 oz. (100 g) fresh ricotta
1 oz. (30 g) unsweetened cocoa powder
Rice flour as needed
Salt

For the sauce:
1 pomegranate
1/4 cup (50 g) cream
3/4 oz. (20 g) butter
Salt
Pepper

1. On a wooden pastry board, mash the potatoes with a potato masher. Add the corn flour, the ricotta and the cocoa powder, and make a well in the centre in which you will break the egg. Season with a pinch of salt and begin to combine all the ingredients without kneading, as the mixture is very delicate and tends to divide.

2. Once smooth and soft, form into a ball. Cut the dough into a few pieces and, on a work surface, roll them into logs of about 1/3 x 4 inches (1 x 10 cm). Use a knife to cut each log into 3/4 inch (2 cm) lengths. Place the gnocchi on trays sprinkled with rice flour so that they do not stick together. Repeat until all the mixture is used up.

3. Scoop out the pomegranate seeds and place them in a bowl. Melt the butter in a non-stick pan over low heat, then add the cream and stir. Add half of the pomegranate seeds and remove from heat. Add salt and pepper to taste.

4. Bring a pot filled with plenty of salted water to the boil. Toss the gnocchi into boiling water, and cook until they float, then fish them out with a skimmer and add them to the pan with the rest of the ingredients. Stir, garnish with the remaining pomegranate seeds and serve immediately.

COCOA TAGLIATELLE

Sausages contain a considerable amount of proteins and of saturated and unsaturated fats. Being gluten-free, they may be considered safe for coeliacs. They are high in energy, and contain minerals such as potassium, calcium and iron. Given their high sodium content, they are not very suitable for people suffering from high blood pressure.

HIGH

4 servings
Preparation time: **40-50 minutes**
Resting time: **24 hours**
Cooking time: **10 minutes**
Calories per serving: **380**

For the tagliatelle:
1/2 cup (70 g) potato starch
3/4 cup (100 g) rice flour
1/3 cup (50 g) cornmeal
1/2 tbsp xanthan gum
4 tbsp (30 g) unsweetened cocoa powder
1 tsp sugar
2 eggs
Water as needed

For the sauce:
1/4 cup (50 g) cream
3 1/2 oz. (100 g) sausage
10 chopped walnuts
Salt
Pepper

1. Put the flours, cocoa powder, eggs and sugar in a bowl. Dissolve the xanthan gum in two tablespoons of water, add it to the rest of the ingredients and knead until smooth and firm. Should the dough be hard and difficult to knead, add a few tablespoons of water a little at a time. Now wrap in cling film and refrigerate for one day.

2. Remove the dough from the fridge and use a rolling pin or a pasta maker to roll it out onto a floured surface (use great care, as the dough is very fragile and tends to fall apart). Roll the pasta dough wafer-thin sheet (1 mm), then lay it out on a kitchen towel sprinkled with rice flour.

3. Flour all the sheets of dough then prepare the tagliatelle with a pasta maker or rolling the dough onto itself and cutting it with a sharp knife. Place the tagliatelle on a floured kitchen towel, well spaced out.

4. Skin the sausage, chop it and cook it in a non-stick pan over low heat for about 5 minutes. Once cooked through, turn off the heat and add the cream and walnuts. Add salt and pepper to taste.

5. Bring a pot filled with plenty of salted water to the boil. Toss in the tagliatelle and cook for 3-4 minutes, then drain. Pour them into the pan with the sauce, stir and serve immediately.

CORNMEAL TAGLIATELLE WITH ARTICHOKES

Parma ham is very easy to digest. It contains water, fats and minerals such as calcium, phosphorus, iron, sodium, potassium, magnesium and zinc, in addition to vitamins B1, B2, B6 and PP. It also has a considerable quantity of protein (about 25-29%).

4 servings
Preparation time: **20 minutes**
Cooking time: **15-20 minutes**
Calories per serving: **360**

12 1/2 oz. (350 g) cornmeal
tagliatelle
4 artichokes
2 cloves of garlic
1 3/4 oz. (50 g) Parma ham
4 tbsp extra virgin olive oil
Salt
Pepper

1. Wash, trim, and snap off the hard, outer leaves of the artichokes, keeping the tender heart. Peel the garlic.

2. Place two tablespoons of oil and the clove of garlic in a non-stick pan. Add the freshly sliced artichokes and cook over low heat to the desired consistency. It is important to slice the artichokes just before cooking, as their leaves tend to oxidise very quickly. Add a few tablespoons of water if needed. Cut the Parma ham into strips.

3. When the artichokes are ready, turn off the heat and add the Parma ham. Add salt and pepper to taste, but keep in mind that the ham can be very salty (so taste it first).

4. Bring a pot filled with plenty of salted water to the boil. Add the tagliatelle and cook for the time indicated on the package, then drain. Add them to the sauce, add two more tablespoons of olive oil, stir and serve.

RICE SPAGHETTI

Rice flour is low in protein but rich in starch, phosphorus and potassium. Rice is the world's most popular food and is the perfect cereal for coeliacs. It is highly digestible, and unpolished is high in B vitamins.

MEDIUM

4 servings
Preparation time: **20 minutes**
Cooking time: **15 minutes**
Calories per serving: **340**

12 1/2 oz. (350 g) rice
spaghetti
2 carrots
3 1/2 oz. (100 g) frozen peas
2 tbsp (20 g) sunflower seeds
2 tbsp (20 g) pumpkin seeds
1 head of lettuce
1/2 cup (100 ml) vegetable
stock
1 tbsp tamari sauce
Salt
Pepper

1. Peel, wash and dry the lettuce. Wrap it in a damp kitchen towel and set aside until ready for use. Peel and wash the carrots, then cut them into strips.

2. In a large non-stick pan, cook the carrots and peas in vegetable stock and tamari sauce over high heat for about 5 minutes. Season with salt and pepper to taste.

3. Toast the sunflower and pumpkin seeds in a separate non-stick pan for a few minutes. Shake the pan to avoid them burning, then keep them aside until ready for use.

4. Bring a pot filled with plenty of salted water to the boil. Add the spaghetti and cook for the time indicated on the package, then drain. Pour the sauce over the spaghetti and stir. Garnish each plate with one or two leaves of lettuce, then add the spaghetti, sprinkle with the toasted seeds, and serve immediately.

SOY NOODLES
WITH VEGETABLES AND PRAWNS

The real tamari sauce is a fermented Japanese soy sauce. It is the only gluten-free form of soy sauce. Buddhist monks, who strictly follow a vegetarian diet, used to use it to add a meaty flavor to their dishes. Its most noteworthy nutritional properties are a high content of antioxidants, 10 times greater than that of red wine, and considerable anti-degenerative and digestive properties. However, its salt content makes it unsuitable for those suffering from high blood pressure and in low-sodium diets.

MEDIUM

4 servings
Preparation time: **10 minutes**
Cooking time: **10 minutes**
Calories per serving: **360**

12 1/2 oz. (350 g) soy noodles
1 yellow bell pepper, small
7 oz. (200 g) Catalogna
chicory
12 prawn tails
5 oz. (150 g) cuttlefish
2 tbsp tamari sauce
3 tbsp sunflower oil
Salt
Pepper
Ginger root to taste (optional)

1. Clean, wash and chop up the pepper. Repeat with the Catalogna chicory. Gut the cuttlefish and wash them well with cold water. Wash the prawns and remove their shells.

2. In a non-stick pan, heat the tamari sauce and two tablespoons of oil then cook the vegetables over high heat for about 5 minutes (adjust the cooking time to the desired consistency). Add salt and pepper to taste (be sure to taste first, as the tamari sauce is quite salty).

3. In a separate non-stick pan, heat one tablespoon of sunflower oil and sauté the cuttlefish over high heat for 1 minute, then add the prawn tails and sauté until they lose their characteristic transparency. Once ready, remove them from heat, add them to the vegetables and set them aside until ready to use.

4. Bring a pot filled with plenty of salted water to the boil. Add the noodles and cook for the time indicated on the package, then drain. Transfer the noodles ointo a serving bowl, add the sauce, stir and serve. If you wish, you can serve each bowl of noodles with a saucer of tamari, seasoned with a few slices of ginger.

CORN PENNE
WITH SHRIMPS AND OREGANO

Shrimps (also known as mantis shrimps, scampi or spot-tail mantis shrimps) are very widespread in the Mediterranean. Like all shellfish, shrimps have a low calorie content and are recommended in low-calorie diets. They contain protein, polyunsaturated fatty acids and B-complex vitamins. They also have the advantage of being easy to digest.

MEDIUM

4 servings
Preparation time: **20 minutes**
Cooking time: **20 minutes**
Calories per serving: **360**

12 1/2 oz. (350 g) corn penne
4 shrimps
4 prawns
4 ripe tomatoes
1 red bell pepper
1 green bell pepper
fresh oregano
4 tbsp extra virgin olive oil
4 cloves of garlic
1 chilli pepper, fresh
Salt

1. Clean, wash and chop the peppers and tomatoes. Peel the garlic. Wash and dry the oregano and chilli pepper.

2. Wash the shrimps, slit the top part of their shell (this will make them easier to peel later) and pat them dry with kitchen paper. Repeat with the prawns.

3. In a non-stick pan, sauté the peppers with oil and the freshly crushed garlic cloves over high heat for 3 to 4 minutes. You can keep some aside as garnish. Add the tomatoes and cook for a further 3 minutes. While cooking, crush the tomatoes with a fork, then add the shrimps and the prawns. Continue cooking over high heat for about 3 minutes, making sure that the sauce does not stick to the pan. When ready, season with freshly sliced chilli and salt to taste.

4. Bring a pot filled with plenty of salted water to the boil. Toss in the penne and cook for the time indicated on the package, then drain, transfer onto the pan with the sauce, and stir. Serve the pasta garnishing each plate with one shrimp and one prawn. Sprinkle with fresh oregano and a few pieces of pepper.

AMATRICIANA REVISITED

Guanciale (cured pork cheek) is rich in protein but also contains 90% saturated and unsaturated fats. It is very stimulating, nutritious and energetic. It is safe for coeliacs as it is gluten-free, and also contains a considerable amount of vitamins and minerals.

4 servings
Preparation time: **15 minutes**
Cooking time: **15 minutes**
Calories per serving: **380**

12 1/2 oz. (350 g) rice
spaghetti
1 3/4 oz. (50 g) guanciale
4 ripe tomatoes
1/3 cup (50 g) grated Pecorino
cheese
1 clove of garlic
Salt
Pepper

1. Wash, slice, seed and peel the tomatoes, keeping the fillets. Drain the excess water in a sieve for 5 minutes. Peel the garlic.

2. Transfer the tomatoes into a bowl and add the garlic so that it releases its flavor. Add salt to taste.

3. Dice the guanciale using a very sharp knife. Brown it in a non-stick pan over high heat for 5 minutes, so that it releases some fat. Once ready, add the tomatoes and cook for 5 more minutes, then turn off the heat and cover.

4. Bring a pot filled with plenty of salted water to the boil. Add the spaghetti and cook for the time indicated on the package, then drain. Add the spaghetti to the sauce, sprinkle with Pecorino cheese and pepper, and stir. Serve hot.

RICE LASAGNE WITH PESTO

Green beans (also known as French beans, string beans, broad beans or baby beans) are the pods of the bean plant, native to America. There are several varieties of these pulses, and they all contain 90% water, making them low-calorie foods. They contain potassium, iron, calcium, vitamins A and C and a considerable amount of easy-to-digest fibre. They perform a purifying action, and are suitable for those suffering from constipation.

HIGH

4 servings
Preparation time: **50 minutes**
Cooking time: **15 minutes**
Resting time: **30 minutes**
Calories per serving: **650**

For the lasagne:
1 cup (150 g) rice flour
1/3 cup (50 g) cornmeal
1/3 cup (50 g) corn flour
1/3 cup (50 g) potato starch
1 tbsp xanthan gum
2 eggs
Water as needed
Olive oil to taste

For the pesto sauce:
1 3/4 oz. (50 g) basil
1/2 cup (100 ml) extra virgin olive oil
2 cloves of garlic
1/2 cup (70 g) Parmesan cheese
4 tbsp (30 g) Pecorino cheese
15 g pine nuts
7 oz. (200 g) green beans, boiled
2 potatoes, boiled and peeled
Salt

1. Preheat the oven to 400° F (200° C) and line a 10-inch (25 cm) baking pan with greaseproof paper .

2. Make a well in the centre of the flours and break the eggs into it. Dissolve the xanthan gum in two tablespoons of water and combine with the rest of the ingredients. Knead until the mixture is soft and smooth.

3. Oil your hands from time to time to keep the dough from sticking. Form the dough into a smooth, firm ball, wrap it in cling film, and let it stand in a cool place for at least 30 minutes, then roll out thin sheets using a pasta maker. Arrange the lasagne on a floured kitchen towel and set aside until ready to use.

4. Gently wash and dry the basil, keeping a few leaves aside as garnish. Peel the garlic and grate the Pecorino and Parmesan cheese.

5. In a mortar, crush the garlic until creamy. Incorporate the basil and pine nuts, then add salt to taste and half of the cheeses. Crush until creamy and smooth. Transfer onto a bowl, then add the oil, the diced potatoes and the freshly chopped green beans. Mix well.

6. Boil the lasagne in salted water and drain halfway through cooking. Arrange a first layer of pasta in the pan, cover it with the pesto sauce, and sprinkle over the grated cheese. Repeat until all the ingredients are used up. Bake for 30 minutes, then remove from the oven. Season with the remaining basil, and serve hot.

RICE TAGLIATELLE WITH QUAILS

Quail meat is high in protein and low in fat. It is a breed of fowl (nowadays mostly raised in farms) that is highly digestible, nutritious and energising, as well as gluten-free.

HIGH

4 servings
Preparation time: **45 minutes**
Cooking time: **15 minutes**
Resting time: **1 hour**
Calories per serving: **320**

For the tagliatelle:
1/2 cup (70 g) rice flour
1/3 cup (50 g) potato starch
1/3 cup (50 g) corn flour
1/3 cup (50 g) cornmeal
1 tbsp xanthan gum
2 eggs
Water as needed

For the sauce:
8 quail breasts
2 tbsp (20 g) pistachio nuts
6 tbsp extra virgin olive oil
Salt
Pepper

1. Pour the flours and eggs into a bowl. Dissolve the xanthan gum in two tablespoons of water, blend with the rest of the ingredients, and knead until smooth and firm. If the dough is too hard and difficult to knead, add a few tablespoons of water a little at a time.

2. Wrap the dough in cling film and let it rest in a cool place for at least one hour.

3. Roll out the dough with a rolling pin or using a pasta maker. Be particularly careful as it is rather fragile and tends to flake. Roll the dough into wafer-thin sheets (1 mm) and arrange them on a floured kitchen towel.

4. Roll up each sheet into a log and cut out the tagliatelle with a sharp knife. Place them on a floured kitchen towel, well spaced out.

5. Heat a non-stick pan with two tablespoons of oil and cook the quail breasts on high heat. From time to time, spray with a tablespoon of water if needed. Continue cooking until the meat is cooked through (approximately 10 minutes). Add salt and pepper to taste.

6. Coarsely chop the pistachios, keeping 1/3 whole as garnish.

7. Bring a pot filled with plenty of salted water to the boil. Toss in the tagliatelle and cook for 3 to 4 minutes, then drain and add them to the sauce. Add four tablespoons of olive oil and the chopped pistachios. Serve garnished with two quail breasts and sprinkle with a few whole pistachio nuts. Serve hot.

COUSCOUS WITH VEGETABLES

The Tropea onion is known for its therapeutic and cleansing properties, given that it is high in phenols, flavonoids, quercetin and minerals such as potassium, sulphur, iron, fluorine, calcium, phosphorus, manganese and zinc. It is rich in vitamins (A, B, C, and E) and can reduce the risk of arterial hypertension and arteriosclerosis. It also helps lower cholesterol levels. Moreover, it contains amny enzymes, and hence is easy to digest.

MEDIUM

4 servings
Preparation time: **20 minutes**
Cooking time: **10 minutes**
Resting time: **5 minutes**
Calories per serving: **350**

1 cup (200 g) rice and corn
couscous
6 celery stalks
7 oz. (200 g) chickpeas,
already soaked
2 courgettes
2 carrots
1 bell pepper
1 Tropea red onion
14 oz. (400 g) peeled
tomatoes, tinned
4 tbsp extra virgin olive oil
Salt
Pepper

1. Clean, wash and dice all the vegetables except the courgettes. Wash and trim the courgettes, then cut them into rounds. Peel and thinly slice the onion.

2. Pour two tablespoons of oil in a large non-stick pan. When the oil is hot, add the onion and fry, then add the vegetables along with the chickpeas and the tomatoes. Cook to the desired consistency, stirring regularly (5 minutes should be enough), then add salt and pepper to taste.

3. Bring a pot filled with 3/4 cup (300 ml) of salted water to the boil. Place the couscous in a large bowl. When the water is boiling, pour it over the couscous, add two tablespoons of olive oil and mix well. Cover and let stand for about 5 minutes, until the couscous absorbs the liquid.

4. Transfer the couscous into separate bowls, add the vegetables, and serve.

PULSE SOUP

Beans are the seeds, contained in pods, of the bean plant. They are rich in protein, fibre, potassium, phosphorus, magnesium, and vitamins B2, B3 and B6. Their high fibre content make them an effective laxative, helping to fight constipation and haemorrhoids.

MEDIUM

4 servings
Preparation time: **25 minutes**
Cooking time: **2 hours**
Resting time: **8 hours**
Calories per serving: **180**

5 oz. (150 g) dried Appaloosa beans
5 oz. (150 g) dried Azuki beans
3 1/2 oz. (100 g) dried chickpeas
2 celery stalks
1 onion
1 clove of garlic
2 tbsp extra virgin olive oil
1 bunch herbs (bay laurel, sage, rosemary)
1/2 cup (100 ml) vegetable stock
2 tbsp extra virgin olive oil
4 small loaves of buckwheat flour bread
Salt
Pepper

1. Soak the beans and chickpeas for about 8 hours, then rinse and drain.

2. Place the herbs in a cheesecloth bag and tie it up with kitchen twine. Wash the celery and chop it into pieces. Peel the garlic and onion, slicing the first thinly and chopping the latter finely. Bring the stock to the boil and keep it warm until ready for use.

3. Heat the oil in a pot, then add the onion, celery and garlic. Fry and stir constantly, then add the pulses, the stock and the herbs. Cook over low heat for about two hours. Add salt and pepper to taste. Stir regularly. If the stock reduces too much, cover and lower the heat. While the soup is cooking, toast the bread.

4. When the soup is ready, turn off the heat, remove the cheesecloth bag with the herbs, and serve. If you wish, you can serve the dish with a drizzle of fresh olive oil, a sprinkling of peppercorns, and toasted buckwheat flour bread.

GRASS PEA SOUP
WITH CHICORY

The grass pea is a pulse similar to the fava bean and chickpea. It is high in protein and starch. It also contains a considerable amount of fibre, while being very low in fat. It is rich in B-complex vitamins (B1, B2 and B3, or PP) and in minerals such as calcium and phosphorus.

EASY

4 servings
Preparation time: **20 minutes**
Cooking time: **2 hours**
Resting time: **8 hours**
Calories per serving: **180**

7 oz. (200 g) dried grass peas
7 oz. (200 g) chicory
1 onion
3 cloves of garlic
2 cups (500 ml) vegetable stock
2 cups (500 ml) water
5 chicory leaves
1 chilli pepper
4 tbsp extra virgin olive oil
Salt
Pepper

1. Soak the grass peas in water for 8 hours, then rinse under running water and drain. Clean and wash the chicory. Peel the garlic cloves and the onion.

2. Heat one tablespoon of oil in a pot and fry the garlic cloves, onion and chicory (keeping about ten leaves aside as garnish). After 2 minutes, add the grass peas, vegetable stock and water. Cook for about 2 hours. Add salt and pepper to taste, then turn off the heat and cover.

3. Finely slice the remaining chicory, then peel and thinly slice the remaining garlic. Wash and cut the chilli into rings. Fry them in a non-stick pan with the remaining oil, and dry off the excess oil with kitchen paper until ready for use (you will use them as garnish).

4. Transfer the hot soup onto individual bowls and sprinkle with the fried garlic, chilli and chicory, then serve.

VEGETABLE, BEAN SPROUT AND QUINOA BROTH

Quinoa is a gluten-free grassy plant native to South America. Its grains are similar to millet. There are many varieties of quinoa, all with considerable nutritional and antioxidant properties. However, the plant is made up by about 10% of fibres that are difficult to digest. It is high in magnesium, sodium, phosphorus, iron and zinc, as well as vitamins A, C, E, and of the B-complex, and amino acids such as lysine and methionine.

MEDIUM

4 servings
Preparation time: **30 minutes**
Cooking time: **3 hours and 15 minutes**
Calories per serving: **140**

3 1/2 oz. (100 g) quinoa
1 celery heart
7 oz. (200 g) fresh beans
3 1/2 oz. (100 g) green beans
300 g red cabbage
3 1/2 oz. (100 g) bean sprouts
1 chilli pepper
1/4 oz. (10 g) fresh coriander

For the stock:
2 celery stalks
1 onion
1 carrot
1 clove of garlic
1/8 oz. (5 g) basil
1/8 oz. (5 g) parsley
Salt

1. Boil the beans for 2 hours, then drain. Now prepare the stock: clean and wash the basil, parsley and vegetables, then chop the latter into small pieces. Place them in a pot and cook in 2 litres of water for 1 hour. Then, strain the stock through a sieve and add salt to taste. Keep the stock warm until ready for use.

2. Put the quinoa in a strainer and rinse it under cold running water to remove any natural residues, then drain well. Place the quinoa in a pot and cover with double the amount of water. Cover the pot with a lid and cook over medium heat, until the water has been completely absorbed (approximately 15 minutes). Set the pot aside, covered, until ready for use. Boil the green beans and wash the coriander, keeping only the leaves.

3. Clean, wash and slice the celery and cabbage. Keep aside one cabbage leaf per person as garnish. In a strainer, rinse the bean sprouts under running water and let them drain for a few minutes. Keep them in a cool place until ready for use.

4. Distribute the quinoa and both the raw and cooked vegetables seasoned with coriander on individual dishes, then pour the hot stock over the dishes. Add freshly sliced chilli and serve.

COCOA PASSATELLI

Soy is composed of 40% protein and 20% saturated and unsaturated fat. It is rich in potassium, phosphorus, calcium and magnesium. In terms of vitamins, it contains A, C and those of the B-complex. It has anti-cancer properties and a protective effect on the intestines, given its high fibre content.

4 servings
Preparation time: **25 minutes**
Cooking time: **4 minutes**
Calories per serving: **460**

1. In a bowl, mash the potatoes with a potato masher, then add the starch, corn and rice flours, egg, cocoa powder and breadcrumbs. Knead for at least 10 minutes, until the dough is pliable, smooth and firm. Form into balls and refrigerate until ready for use.

2. In a non-stick pan, heat the cream over very low heat. Meanwhile, crush the hazelnuts in a mortar, then blend with the cream, and stir. Add salt and pepper to taste, then turn off the heat.

3. Bring a pot filled with plenty of salted water to the boil, then force each ball of dough through a potato ricer directly into the boiling water. Cook for 2 to 3 minutes, then drain the passatelli and incorporate them into the sauce. Stir, and serve hot.

For the passatelli:
1 lb. 2 oz. (500 g) potatoes, boiled
1/3 cup (50 g) potato starch
1/3 cup (50 g) corn flour
1 cup (100 g) rice flour
breadcrumbs
1 egg
4 tbsp (30 g) unsweetened cocoa powder

For the sauce:
1/2 cup (100 g) soy cream
4 tbsp (40 g) toasted hazelnuts
Salt
Pepper

OCTOPUS AND PEA RISOTTO

The octopus is a mollusc high in potassium, calcium and phosphorus. It is also rich in vitamins A and B1, as well as in protein and retinol. Due to its high water content, it is suitable for low-calorie diets. Some people find it hard to digest due to its protein-rich connective tissue.

EASY

4 servings
Preparation time: **15 minutes**
Cooking time: **15-20 minutes**
Calories per serving: **380**

7 oz. (200 g) rice
7 oz. (200 g) octopus, boiled
3 1/2 oz. (100 g) cherry tomatoes
3 1/2 oz. (100 g) orange cherry tomatoes
3 1/2 oz. (100 g) fresh or frozen peas
1 cup (200 ml) vegetable stock, hot
1 bunch herbs (dried oregano, parsley, and fresh Greek basil, a small-leaved variety)
1 shallot
2 tbsp extra virgin olive oil
Salt
Freshly ground pepper

1. Peel the shallot and chop it finely. Wash and cut the tomatoes in half.

2. In a non-stick pan, heat the oil and sauté the shallot over high heat for 2 minutes, then add the peas and the tomatoes. Rinse the rice several times in cold water, then drain.

3. Cut the octopus into small pieces and add it to the rest of the ingredients. Add salt and pepper to taste.

4. Put the rice in a pot containing 1 litre of water, and bring it to the boil. Cook on low heat for 12 minutes, covered. When it has reached the desired consistency, turn off the heat and drain. Transfer onto the pan with the sauce, stir and cook for a few more minutes, until all the ingredients have blended together.

5. Spray with the stock, and cook for a further 3 minutes, stirring regularly, then turn off the heat. Arrange the rice on a dish, sprinkle with herbs, season with freshly ground pepper, and serve.

SEAFOOD PAELLA WITH WHOLE GRAIN RICE

Saffron, usually sold in its powdered form, is a very special spice indeed, as its cost per gram is higher than that of gold. It is made up of 12% water and 65% carbohydrates. In terms of minerals, it contains calcium, phosphorus, sodium, potassium, iron, magnesium and manganese. Saffron acts as a stimulant and antidepressant. Moreover, it is rich in vitamins A, C and of the B-complex, as well as antioxidants and anti-degenerative substances like lycopenes and zeaxanthin.

MEDIUM

4 servings
Preparation time: **30 minutes**
Cooking time: **15 minutes**
Resting time: **30 minutes**
Calories per serving: **380**

7 oz. (200 g) whole grain rice
8 scampi
1 lb. 2 oz. (500 g) mussels
3 1/2 oz. (100 g) squid
1 lemon
1 bell pepper
7 oz. (200 g) peas
1 onion
2 tbsp oil
2 cups (500 ml) vegetable stock, hot
1 sachet saffron
2 tbsp extra virgin olive oil
Salt
Pepper

1. Rinse the whole grain rice and boil in 1 litre of salted water for 20 minutes. Turn off the heat, drain and keep aside until ready for use.

2. Soak the mussels in water with one tablespoon of salt for about 30 minutes, shaking them from time to time. Discard any mussels that have broken or opened. Scrape the rest with an iron brush and remove the beard. Wash and gut the squid, then cut into rounds. Wash the scampi.

3. Rinse the mussels and leave them to drain for a few minutes. Place them into a non-stick pan and cook over medium heat until they open. Remove them from the heat and let them stand, covered.

4. Remove the pepper's stalk, seeds and white parts, then slice them into strips. Wash and slice the lemon. Peel the onion and slice it thinly. Heat two tablespoons of oil in a non-stick pan and sauté the onion. Add the vegetables and cook until tender (approximately 10 minutes). Add the rice, stir and cook for a further 10 minutes, stirring regularly with a wooden spoon and spraying, if necessary, with the stock. Add salt and pepper to taste. Dissolve the saffron in half a cup of stock.

5. Now add the mussels, squid, scampi and saffron. Cook for 3 to 4 minutes, until they have reached the desired consistency, then remove from heat. Arrange the rice on individual dishes and add two scampi per person. Garnish with lemon slices, and serve.

WITH LARGELY GLUTEN- AND CEREAL-FREE MAIN COURSES, COELIACS CAN FINALLY FEEL SAFE. AND IF THEY JUST CAN'T GIVE UP ON CRISPY BREADING, FRIED FISH OR TEMPURA, THEN THEY CAN REPLACE FLOUR WITH POTATO STARCH, CORNMEAL OR RICE FLOUR.

It is easy to avoid gluten when preparing main courses: simply cook vegetables, fish and meat (chicken, beef fillets, steaks, turkey, etc.) using techniques such as grilling or steaming, and ignore all recipes that require wheat flour. But there are a number of tricks you can adopt to make potato pancakes, stuffed cuttlefish, chicken nuggets and irresistibly crispy fries.

By grinding rice, corn or buckwheat bread, for example, you can get excellent breadcrumbs, and by crumbling or coarsely chopping corn breadsticks, you can obtain a beautifully crunchy breading. What about tempura batter, I hear you ask? Instead of common wheat flour, simply use cornmeal, rice flour or potato starch. The result will be a very light, almost impalpable batter, beautifully white in colour, that will envelop your ingredients without weighing them down with too many fats. Rice flour, as well as preserving the food's moisture, also absorbs little cooking oil, making it ideal for classic fried fish: your dish will be lighter, less greasy, extremely tasty and delightfully crunchy. The flavors will not mix, and the taste of oil will not prevail over all others. And that's not all: rice flour is very easy to digest, even for those who suffer from gluten intolerance.

The preparation of pancakes, meatballs and timbales is by no means penalised by the ban on wheat flour. If anything, you can choose between the impalpable texture of cornmeal and potato starch and the rougher one of rice flour. The former are certainly better for velvety smooth mashed potatoes, but are not recommended for coating meat: in this case, rice or corn flour are best,

MAIN COURSES

and are sold either finely or very finely ground. The latter is perfect for creams and to thicken sauces.

The kitchen is one of those places in which to give free reign to the imagination. It is possible to prepare recipes seemingly out of bounds for coeliacs and those with a gluten intolerance, by replacing, integrating and revolutionising their ingredients: wheat can be replaced with rice, and breadcrumbs with corn breadsticks, perhaps soaked in water to make them suitable, for example, as a stuffing for cuttlefish. On the other hand, for those dishes that have always been permitted, such as all forms of polenta, there is nothing we need suggest to improve their digestibility: these are perfect just as they are.

QUINOA BALLS
WITH FLAX AND SESAME SEEDS

Flax is a grassy plant, the seeds of which are high in omega-3 fatty acids, dietary minerals, proteins, lipids, linoleic acid and fibres. They have significant antioxidant properties and also help improve blood circulation. Omega-3 has a healthy effect on the heart, and a spoonful of flax seeds contains as many as 1.7 grams! It is thought that flax seeds may reduce the risk of developing breast, prostate and colon cancer.

EASY

4 servings
Preparation time: **20 minutes**
Cooking time: **4 minutes**
Calories per serving: **450**

1 cup (200 g) quinoa, cooked
3 tbsp (30 g) flax seeds
3 tbsp (30 g) sesame seeds
3 1/2 oz. (100 g) ricotta
1/3 cup (50 g) rice flour
2 tbsp herbs (oregano, thyme, coriander and cardamom)
3/4 cup plus 1 tbsp (200 ml) peanut oil
Salt
Pepper

1. Pour the quinoa, ricotta cheese, herbs and pepper into a bowl, and knead with your hands until the mixture is smooth.

2. Prepare some balls by taking a little of the mixture at a time and rolling it into a ball with your hands. Repeat until all the mixture is used up.

3. Place the two types of seeds on a large plate, keeping them separate, and roll some balls in the flax seeds and the others in the sesame seeds. Press lightly so that the seeds adhere to the surface and do not disperse while cooking.

4. Dip the balls in flour, then heat the oil in a large frying pan and, when hot, fry the well-floured meatballs for 3-4 minutes, turning and shaking them often in the pan.

5. When browned and crispy, remove them from the pan and dry off the excess oil with kitchen paper. Transfer them onto a serving dish, add salt and pepper to taste, then serve.

NUT AND CAPRINO CHEESE NUGGETS

Goat's cheese is very easy to digest, even for those who are intolerant to the casein typical of cow's milk cheeses, or do not produce sufficient enzymes required for its digestion. They contain complete proteins and various minerals, such as calcium, magnesium and, to a lesser extent, phosphorus. They are useful to stimulate brain activity, being rich in B-complex vitamins.

EASY

4 servings
Preparation time: **15 minutes**
Calories per serving: **180**

8 3/4 oz. (250 g) fresh
Caprino cheese
1 oz. (25 g) pistachio nuts
1 oz. (25 g) hazelnuts from
Piedmont
1 head lettuce, cleaned
Salt
Pepper

1. Pour the cheese into a bowl, add salt and pepper to taste, then work it with a fork until the mixture is smooth.

2. Prepare some balls by taking a little of the mixture at a time and rolling it into a ball with your hands. Repeat until all the ingredients are used up. Arrange the balls on a plate.

3. In a mortar, finely ground the pistachios and hazelnuts separately.

4. Place the two types of nuts onto separate plates and roll half the balls in the pistachios and the other half in the hazelnuts.

5. Place the balls on a platter, perhaps arranged on a bed of lettuce, and serve.

POLENTA IN A TOMATO SAUCE

Corn polenta is traditionally believed to be an aphrodisiac. The flour with which it is prepared undoubtedly contains less carbohydrate than wheat flour, despite being rich in easily digestible starches. While this dish is suitable for coeliacs, it must be remembered that it is high in calories and low in vitamins and proteins.

4 servings
Preparation time: **10 minutes**
Cooking time: **20 minutes**
Calories per serving: **600**

14 oz. (400 g) polenta, ready to serve
14 oz. (400 g) peeled tomatoes
7 oz. (200 g) sausage
1 clove of garlic
1 shallot
4 sprigs fresh rosemary
4 sage leaves
2 tbsp extra virgin olive oil
Salt
Pepper

1. Peel and chop the garlic and shallot. Wash, dry and mince the rosemary, setting aside some leaves as garnish. Wash the sage and set it aside. Drain and chop the peeled tomatoes.

2. In a non-stick pan, sauté the garlic and shallots in two tablespoons of olive oil for 5 minutes over high heat. Add the tomatoes and minced rosemary, then stir. Cut the sausages into small pieces and cook them with the tomatoes for about 10 minutes, stirring often. Add salt and pepper to taste. When cooked, remove from heat and let stand, covered with a lid.

3. Cut the polenta into eight slices, then heat them in a non-stick pan for 5 minutes over high heat, being careful not to burn them. Once hot, serve two slices of polenta per person, along with the sausage and tomato sauce. Decorate the dish with the rosemary and sage.

RICE AND VEGETABLE TIMBALE

Peas are popularly considered nutritionally poor legumes, but they are in fact rich in protein. They also contain significant amounts of minerals such as iron, potassium and calcium, as well as vitamins C and of the B-complex.

4 servings
Preparation time: **15 minutes**
Cooking time: **40 minutes**
Calories per serving: **480**

10 1/2 oz. (300 g) rice
3 tomatoes
5 oz. (150 g) spinach, cooked and drained
3 1/2 oz. (100 g) peas
1 shallot
1 l vegetable stock, hot
1/4 cup. (30 g) rice or corn breadcrumbs
2 tbsp extra virgin olive oil
Salt
Pepper

1. Wash, slice, seed and peel the tomatoes, keeping the fillets.

2. Preheat the oven to 400° F (200° C). Peel and slice the shallot, then sauté it in a non-stick pan with two tablespoons of olive oil for about 5 minutes, over high heat. Add the rice and toast it lightly (for about 2 minutes), stirring with a wooden spoon.

3. Add the tomato fillets, spinach and peas to the rice, then stir. Cook for about 15 minutes, spraying regularly with the stock as the rice dries. Salt and pepper to taste.

4. Arrange a thin layer of rice or corn breadcrumbs on the bottom of a baking tray lined with greaseproof paper, then pour in the mixture. Using a spatula, give the mixture a compact shape, then sprinkle the surface with more breadcrumbs, so as to form a golden crust while cooking.

5. Bake for about 20 minutes, then let the timbale cool slightly at room temperature. Turn out the timbale and slice it on a serving platter. Serve it hot or at room temperature.

VEGETABLE AND PRAWN TEMPURA

Prawns are shellfish that contain about 15% protein, while fats and sugars are present in very low concentrations. Their low calorie content, therefore, makes them attractive to dieters. However, it is important not to go overboard with the seasonings. Prawns also contain a substance that has recently come under the spotlight in nutraceutics: astaxanthin, a bioflavonoid believed to significantly prevent the ageing of tissues and damage caused by vascular diseases in terms of microcirculation.

4 servings
Preparation time: **10 minutes**
Cooking time: **2 minutes**
Calories per serving: **580**

2 courgettes
1 red bell pepper
1 green bell pepper
12 prawns
3/4 cup (100 g) corn flour
1/3 cup (50 g) rice flour
300 ml sparkling water, ice cold
1 1/4 cup (300 ml) peanut oil
Salt
Pepper

1. Trim, wash and cut the courgettes into wafer-thin sheet slices (about 1 mm). Clean and wash the peppers, then chop them into small strips.

2. Rinse the prawns under running water and gently pat them dry with kitchen paper.

3. Pour the flours and water into a bowl, then stir with a whisk until smooth and free of lumps. Heat the oil in a non-stick pan to 340° F (170° C).

4. Cover the vegetables and prawns in the batter a few at a time, then dip them into the hot oil. Fry for about 2 minutes or until crisp and lightly browned.

5. Remove the fried vegetables and prawns a little at a time with a skimmer and dry off the excess oil with kitchen paper, then transfer them onto a serving dish. Add salt and pepper to taste, then serve.

MIXED FISH FRY

This dish is made with a mixture of small fish (sole, red mullet, cod, grey mullet, anchovies, sardines, and so on) known as Paranza in Italian. These fish varieties are easy to digest and are a good source of protein and omega-3 fatty acids, with considerable nourishing and antioxidant properties.

EASY

4 servings
Preparation time: **15 minutes**
Cooking time: **15-20 minutes**
Calories per serving: **480**

1 lb. 2 oz. (500 g) shrimps
7 oz. (200 g) hake fillets, cleaned
10 1/2 oz. (300 g) anchovies
14 oz. (400 g) sardines
3/4 cup (100 g) rice flour
2 lemons
1 1/4 cup (300 ml) sunflower oil
Salt

1. Slit the underside of the shrimps and rinse them under running water, then pat them dry with kitchen paper. Cut off the head of the anchovies and sardines, and gut them. Then, wash and pat them dry with kitchen paper.

2. Wash the lemons. Dip the anchovies, sardines, shrimps and hake fillets in flour, making sure they are fully coated.

3. Heat the oil in a non-stick pan to 340° F (170° C). Dip the ingredients into the oil, starting with the hake and ending with the sardines. Let them fry for about 3-4 minutes, gently moving the pieces but turning them only when you are sure that the fish and shellfish have become fairly firm. Let them cook until they form a golden crust.

4. When cooked, remove the fried fish and shellfish with a skimmer, drain the excess oil with kitchen paper, and transfer them onto a serving dish. Garnish with freshly cut lemon segments, then season with salt to taste. Serve hot.

POTATO PANCAKES

Black pepper is the unripe fruit of the Piper nigrum *plant, which takes on its characteristic dark colour when sun dried. In addition to providing an unmistakable aroma, pepper contains minerals such as iron, calcium, sodium, potassium, phosphorus and zinc, as well as vitamins C, E and of the B-complex. It is best to use freshly ground pepper, in order to enjoy its flavor to the full.*

4 servings
Preparation time: **20 minutes**
Cooking time: **35 minutes**
Calories per serving: **300**

1 3/4 lb. (800 g) potatoes
4 tbsp (30 g) Parmesan cheese
1 egg
1/3 cup (50 g) corn flour
2 tbsp parsley, dried
4 tbsp olive oil
Salt
Black peppercorns

1. Cook the potatoes in boiling water for about 30 minutes, then drain and leave to cool before peeling. Pour the corn flour into a shallow dish.

2. In a bowl, mash the potatoes until soft using a potato masher. Add the egg, the Parmesan cheese, half the parsley and a generous sprinkling of ground pepper, then mix well to combine all the ingredients together.

3. Prepare some balls by rolling a little of the mixture at a time with your hands, then flatten them slightly between your palms. Roll them in the corn flour, ensuring they are well coated, so as to protect the pancakes while cooking and prevent them from breaking up.

4. Heat the oil in a non-stick pan, then fry the pancakes for 4-5 minutes, turning them several times to brown them evenly.

5. Remove them from the pan with a skimmer and dry the excess oil by placing the pancakes on a plate covered with kitchen paper. Let them stand for a few minutes, then add salt to taste. Transfer the pancakes onto a serving dish, sprinkle with the remaining dried parsley, and serve.

FRIED SARDINES IN A RICE CRUST

Sardines contain complete proteins, omega-3 fatty acids and essential minerals such as phosphorus, which is crucial for balanced physical and mental development. They are highly nutritious, and help keep the blood vessels and heart healthy.

EASY

4 servings
Preparation time: **10 minutes**
Cooking time: **10-15 minutes**
Calories per serving: **480**

14 oz. (400 g) sardines
1/2 cup (70 g) rice flour
3/4 cup plus 1 tbsp (200 ml) soybean oil
Salt
1 lemon (optional)

1. Gut the sardines and remove the head. Rinse them under running water and gently pat them dry with kitchen paper.

2. Dip each sardine in flour, making sure they are fully coated.

3. Heat the oil in a non-stick pan to 340° F (170° C), then fry the fish for about 3-4 minutes, turning them a few times.

4. When the sardines are fried and crispy, remove them from the pan with a skimmer and dry the excess oil by placing them on a plate covered with kitchen paper. Transfer them onto a serving dish, season with salt, and serve. If you wish, you can garnish the dish with the lemon, cut into segments.

STUFFED CUTTLEFISH

Cuttlefish are easy to digest and are rich in essential minerals (phosphorus, potassium and calcium), as well as vitamins A, D and B1, fibres, and polyunsaturated fatty acids. The latter keep cholesterol under control and improve blood circulation.

MEDIUM

4 servings
Preparation time: **35 minutes**
Cooking time: **20 minutes**
Calories per serving: **295**

8 small cuttlefish, cleaned
7 oz. (200 g) corn breadsticks
2 eggs
1 orange
1 orange chilli pepper
1 red chilli pepper
1 dried chilli pepper
1 tsp paprika
1 bunch fresh parsley
4 sprigs lemon verbena
Salt

1. Preheat the oven to 400° F (200° C). Finely chop the breadsticks in the blender. Clean, wash and dry the parsley, then chop half, keeping the rest aside as garnish. Wash the fresh chilli peppers and the lemon verbena. Chop a few leaves of the latter to flavor some of the cuttlefish, and keep the rest aside as garnish.

2. Pour the chopped breadsticks and the eggs into a bowl. Mix the ingredients well, then season with salt to taste.

3. Chop the dried chilli and mix it with the paprika. Divide the cuttlefish stuffing into two: add the chopped parsley to one half and the paprika and chilli mix to the other. Stuff half the cuttlefish with one type of filling and the other half with the other. Bake for about 20 minutes.

4. Once cooked, take the dish out of the oven and sprinkle the cuttlefish with the remaining parsley and a few lemon verbena leaves. Slice the red and orange chilli peppers into rings, and sprinkle one type over half the cuttlefish and the other type over the other half.

5. Wash and slice the orange. Arrange the slices on a platter and lay the cuttlefish on top. Garnish the dish with the remaining lemon verbena, and serve.

STUFFED SQUID

Squid is a mollusc related to the cuttlefish and octopus. Its meat is firmer and more flexible, and therefore easier to stuff. It is low in fat, and is also a good source of proteins. It is rich in minerals, such as sodium, potassium, calcium, phosphorus, iron and iodine, and also contains micronutrients such as selenium and zinc. Its main vitamins are A and those of the B-complex. Be very careful when buying squid: it must be extremely fresh, as its fkesh deteriorates quickly, losing its remarkable nutritional properties and flavor.

MEDIUM

4 servings
Preparation time: **25 minutes**
Cooking time: **20 minutes**
Calories per serving: **230**

8 squid, medium-sized
14 oz. (400 g) tomato purée
1 oz. (30 g) parsley, fresh
3 1/2 oz. (100 g) corn bread
for the stuffing
4 slices corn bread
as an accompaniment
1 potato, boiled
2 eggs
1/3 cup (50 g) seasoned
ricotta, grated
1/2 cup (100 ml) vegetable
stock
2 cloves of garlic
2 tbsp oil
Salt
Pepper

1. Pull off the squid's tentacles (you can keep them aside and use them for a pasta sauce, for example) and remove the entrails, then wash the squid several times. Put it in a colander and store in the refrigerator until ready for use. Wash the parsley leaves, keeping a few leaves aside as garnish, then chop them on a wooden chopping board.

2. Break up the bread for the stuffing, and soak it in warm vegetable stock. When swollen and soft, transfer it into a sieve, press it with your hands and reduce it to a ductile mass, without however squeezing out all the liquid.

3. Mash the potatoes with a fork and pour into a bowl, then add the eggs, ricotta, bread, chopped parsley and a tablespoon of tomato purée. Add salt and pepper to taste. Mix well until the mixture is smooth and the flavors have combined.

4. Stuff the squid about three-quarters full, then close the molluscs with a toothpick so that the filling does not spill out during cooking.

5. Crush the garlic cloves without peeling them, and put them in a pan with the oil. When browned, remove them and pour the rest of the tomato sauce into the pan. Salt to taste and let thicken for 5 minutes, then add the squid. Cover and cook over medium heat for 5 minutes, then turn the squid and check that the sauce has not dried up: if necessary, add a few tablespoons of hot water. Continue cooking for about 3 minutes, then remove the pan from heat and arrange the squid on a dish, flavoring it with the sauce. Add a few pieces of corn bread per serving, garnish with the remaining parsley, and serve hot.

SPICY TURKEY NUGGETS

Turkey is a white meat rich in proteins and amino acids, especially tryptophan, which is highly digestible. It also contains an appreciable amount of iron, in concentrations similar to those of red meat. Moreover, it is a high energy meat that is low in saturated fat.

EASY

4 servings
Preparation time: **25 minutes**
Cooking time: **5 minutes**
Calories per serving: **250**

1. Keep the quinoa warm. In a small bowl, mix the curry with the minced chilli. Cut the turkey breast into smallish pieces, then roll these in the spices, lightly pressing the meat with your hands to coat it completely.

2. In a non-stick pan, fry the nuggets in oil over medium heat for about 5 minutes, spraying regularly with wine. Add salt to taste.

3. In another non-stick pan, toast the pine nuts, then add them to the nuggets (keep one third by as garnish).

4. Distribute the quinoa on individual dishes and place the nuggets on top. Add salt to taste. Garnish each plate with the remaining pine nuts, and serve.

14 oz. (400 g) turkey breast
5 tbsp (30 g) curry
1 dried chilli pepper, minced
3/4 oz. (20 g) pine nuts
1 cup (200 g) quinoa, cooked
1 glass white wine
2 tbsp extra virgin olive oil
Salt

CORN BREADED
CHICKEN NUGGETS

White meat boasts highly digestible proteins. It is excellent in fighting fatigue, increasing antibodies and renewing tissues. Chicken breast, in particular, contains 75% water and 23% protein, while fats make up less than 1% of the total weight. It is also a good source of vitamins A, C, E and of the B-complex, and of minerals such as magnesium, zinc, copper, selenium, potassium and iron.

4 servings
Preparation time: **20 minutes**
Cooking time: **15 minutes**
Calories per serving: **280**

14 oz. (400 g) chicken breast
5 oz. (150 g) corn breadsticks
1/3 cup (50 g) cornmeal
1 egg
Salt
Freshly ground pepper

1. Chop up the chicken breast. Finely grind the breadsticks in the blender. Preheat the oven to 400° F (220° C).

2. In a bowl, mix the flour with the crushed breadsticks, then season with salt and pepper to taste. Break the egg into a bowl and beat it until the egg white and yolk are well mixed.

3. Dip each nugget in the egg wash, then roll it in the flour until fully coated, pressing with your hands to ensure it adheres well.

4. Arrange the nuggets on a baking sheet lined with greaseproof paper and cook in the oven for 5 minutes; then, remove them from the oven, turn the pieces round, and put them back into the oven. Cook them for another 10 minutes, and take them out of the oven when golden brown. Let them cool for 2 minutes before transferring them onto a serving dish. Season with freshly ground pepper, and serve.

CITRUS CHICKEN

All citrus fruits are rich in vitamins A and E, the latter being a powerful antioxidant. However, they are especially high in vitamin C, a substance with significant anti-tumour properties that can also prevent influenza and osteoporosis, as well as improving blood coagulation and boosting the immune system. Being acidic, citrus fruits are contraindicated in those suffering from ulcer.

EASY

4 servings
Preparation time: **20 minutes**
Cooking time: **10 minutes**
Calories per serving: **250**

1. Pour the flours into a bowl and mix well. Roll the chicken pieces in this mixture, pressing gently to ensure the flour fully coats the meat.

2. In a non-stick pan, fry the chicken in oil over medium heat for about 10 minutes, turning several times. Towards the end, add the freshly squeezed juice of an orange and lemon, then add salt and pepper to taste.

3. Wash and slice the remaining lemon and orange. Wash and dry the hyssop.

4. Place the chicken in individual dishes and garnish at will with slices of orange and lemon and a few sprigs of hyssop. Serve hot.

4 chicken thighs,
cut into 4 pieces
3 tbsp (30 g) rice flour
4 tbsp (30 g) potato starch
2 lemons
2 oranges
3 tbsp extra virgin olive oil
4 sprigs hyssop
Salt
Pepper

FRIED PHEASANT
WITH APPLES

The white meat of pheasant, which is rich in vitamins B1, B2 and B3 (or PP), is made up of 25% proteins, essential for growth, and of fibres, that are much easier to digest than those of other white and red meats. Therefore, it is particularly suitable for children.

MEDIUM

4 servings
Preparation time: **15 minutes**
Cooking time: **60 minutes**
Calories per serving: **250**

1 pheasant, cut into pieces
(approximately 1 kg)
4 red apples
3 sprigs fresh rosemary
1 shallot
1 glass white wine
Cornmeal as needed
2 tbsp extra virgin olive oil
Salt
Pepper

1. Clean the pheasant of any feathers, then wash and dry it thoroughly with kitchen paper. Peel the shallot and slice it thinly. Wash and dry the rosemary. Wash the apples, but don't peel them.

2. In a non-stick pan, brown the meat with the oil and shallots, then add the wine. Let the alcohol evaporate, reduce the heat to low, and cook for about an hour, turning the pieces from time to time to brown them evenly. Halfway through cooking, cut the apples into wedges, leaving the skin on, and add them to the pheasant. Season with salt and pepper to taste, and stir occasionally with a wooden spoon.

3. When cooked, strain the gravy, mix in a teaspoon of cornmeal, and let it thicken in a saucepan. Arrange the pheasant and apples on a dish, garnish with the rosemary, and serve with the cornmeal gravy.

BEEF FILLET

Beef, in other words the meat of an uncastrated male bovine or of a female bovine that has never given birth, is rich in complete proteins, including plenty of myoglobin and hemoglobin, as well as being high in precious minerals. While less rich in water than veal, it is equally digestible and even more nutritious: better not to eat too much, so as not to overload on saturated fat.

4 servings
Preparation time: **10 minutes**
Cooking time: **8 minutes**
Calories per serving: **180**

1. On a large plate, wet the sheets of rice individually in cold water, and let them soften for 2 minutes. Take them off the plate and dry off the excess water with a cotton cloth. Heat a griddle or non-stick pan over high heat.

2. Wrap the sheets of rice around the edge of each fillet. Tie it with kitchen twine or natural raffia.

3. Cook the fillet on the griddle for about 3-4 minutes per side, or until the meat is cooked to your liking.

4. When cooked, arrange the fillets on a serving dish, add salt and pepper to taste, and, if you wish, season with olive oil (remember that a spoonful of oil is equivalent to 90 calories). Serve the meat hot.

4 beef fillets (5 oz./150 g each)
4 rice sheets
Black Hawaiian salt
Pepper
4 tbsp extra virgin olive oil
(optional)

VEGETABLE OMELETTE ROLL

Egg is rich in fat and protein, but also in lecithin, widely appreciated for its health benefits, and in particular its ability to increase "good cholesterol" and reduce "bad cholesterol" levels in the blood. Many of the fats it contains are unsaturated, and therefore useful for the cardiovascular system. However, caution must be exercised in the presence of gallstones and liver diseases.

MEDIUM

4 servings
Preparation time: **20 minutes**
Cooking time: **30 minutes**
Calories per serving: **180**

For the roll:
4 eggs
2 tbsp Parmesan, grated
1/3 cup (50 ml) sparkling water
Salt
Pepper

For the filling:
2 courgettes
2 carrots
1 red bell pepper
3/4 oz. (20 g) green olives
2 tbsp extra virgin olive oil
Salt
Pepper

1. Preheat the oven to 320° F (160° C). Trim, wash and slice the courgettes into rounds. Trim, peel and chop the carrots into small pieces. Remove the stalk, seeds and white parts of the pepper, then chop it into chunks. Pit the olives and cut them into rounds.

2. In a non-stick pan, let the vegetables simmer in oil with the olives for about 10 minutes (or until they have reached the desired consistency), stirring occasionally. Add salt and pepper to taste. When ready, cover the pan and leave the vegetables to stand.

3. Break the eggs into a bowl, add the Parmesan cheese, and season with salt and pepper to taste. Add the water, and stir until the mixture is smooth. Pour it into a rectangular baking dish lined with greaseproof paper, and bake for about 20 minutes.

4. When cooked, remove the dish from the oven, gently turn the omelette out, and place it on a chopping board. Place the vegetables on top, and roll the omelette on itself so as to obtain a stuffed cylinder.

5. Wrap the roll in cling film and leave it to cool slightly, then remove the cling film, slice and serve.

OCTOPUS WITH POTATOES

Parsley contains 50% sugar, 26% protein, and 6% water. The rest is made up of fibres and minerals (calcium, potassium, sodium, phosphorus, magnesium, iron, zinc, selenium and manganese). It includes vitamins A, C, E, K and of the B-complex, in addition to being a good source of amino acids. Parsley also contains a substantial amount of antioxidant bioflavonoids. The latter can delay cellular ageing and reduce the risk of various types of cancers.

MEDIUM

4 servings
Preparation time: **40 minutes**
Cooking time: **50 minutes**
Calories per serving: **270**

1 octopus (approximately 1 kg)
14 oz. (400 g) potatoes, small
1 clove of garlic
1 sprig parsley
1 lemon
2 tbsp extra virgin olive oil
Salt
Pepper

1. Thoroughly wash the octopus so as to remove any residues of sand. Remove the beak and entrails.

2. Bring 1 litre of water to the boil in a pot, and add the whole octopus for about 30 minutes (or until it reaches the desired consistency).

3. Meanwhile, boil the whole potatoes in plenty of water for about 15-20 minutes, then drain them and place them on a chopping board. When they have cooled down slightly, peel them and cut them into thirds or quarters, depending on their size.

4. When the octopus is cooked, remove it from the water, place it on a chopping board, and let it drain and cool slightly. Then, cut it into pieces with a sharp knife or scissors. Transfer the pieces into a bowl.

5. Clean, wash, dry and mince the parsley. Peel and mince the garlic.

6. Combine all the ingredients (octopus, potatoes, parsley and garlic), then drizzle over the olive oil and freshly squeezed lemon juice. Season with salt and pepper to taste, then stir and serve.

VEGETABLES FILL THE TABLE WITH COLOUR AND DELICIOUS GLUTEN-FREE DISHES. SO UNLEASH YOUR IMAGINATION TO PREPARE COUNTLESS SALADS AND STUFFED VEGETABLES. FOR BREADING AND BATTERS, SIMPLY USE POTATO STARCH AND RICE, CORN OR BUCKWHEAT FLOURS.

Side dishes are mainly made with seasonal vegetables, either raw, cooked, preserved in oil, seasoned with sauces, or steamed: there is something for everyone, including those who, like coeliacs, have to deal with food restrictions. Indeed, there is no limit to the daily use of vegetables, except in the case of allergies to specific foods.

In general, vegetables are safe to eat, but it is important to pay attention to what they are served with, for example wheat, spelt, kamut or barley salads, and purées or oatmeal creams (it seems that the majority of coeliacs can tolerate this cereal, but as a precaution it would be better to take no risks, and not to include it in a gluten-free diet). And let's not forget that rye is out of bounds too. So what can coeliacs eat? A ratatouille with aubergine, tomato, peppers and celery, or with roasted vegetables, is totally risk free. The same may be said for a nice plate of crunchy baked peppers, as long as they are coated in millet breadcrumbs. The first step for coeliacs to adopt a healthy diet is to empty the pantry, throwing away anything that might be dangerous. It is best to err on the side of caution, and to discard anything that poses a risk, no matter how small. This may seem obvious, but it is important for coeliacs to understand that it is only by accepting their difference that they can hope to regain their wellbeing. They can fill the pantry with the flours they are allowed to eat, and unleash their imagination, inventing and preparing countless tasty yet healthy dishes.

SIDE DISHES

Remember that dietary restrictions do not preclude all that is tasty. You just need to be discerning about the temptations that come your way. Vegetables can be served raw, steamed, or perhaps flavored by a tasty béchamel made from corn flour or potato starch, according to your taste – there's nothing better on cauliflower or broccoli. To make a truly special dish, you can dip some artichokes, for example, in a light and tasty batter made with rice or corn flour. Make sure you stir this continuously in the making, as it tends to divide and form a firm layer that settles on the bottom of the bowl. Appropriately stirred, however, it will coat your vegetables to perfection, providing added flavor and texture. The end result will be surprisingly balanced, despite what you might think during preparation.

RATATOUILLE

The aubergine, a berry from the nightshade family, is very rich in water, contains little sugar and is high in fibre and potassium. It has a low calorie content, and therefore makes the perfect food for a healthy diet, as it is fat free and high in water. It provides a good intake of vitamins, especially of the A and C groups, and has a slightly spicy flavor. The cleansing, diuretic and digestive properties of aubergines, stimulate liver and gallbladder activity.

4 servings
Preparation time: **15 minutes**
Cooking time: **20 minutes**
Calories per serving: **120**

1 aubergine
2 tomatoes
1 red bell pepper, small
4 celery stalks
1 white onion
20 black olives (e.g. Gaeta olives)
4 garlic cloves, whole
2 spicy chilli peppers, fresh
2 tbsp extra virgin olive oil
2 basil leaves
Salt

1. Clean and wash the vegetables, then cut the into the desired shapes.

2. Grease a non-stick pan with oil and stew the vegetables over medium heat for 5 minutes. Season with salt and reduce the heat to low. Add the olives, a whole crushed garlic clove (unpeeled) and the freshly sliced chilli peppers. Cover with a lid and continue cooking.

3. Clean, wash and dry the basil.

4. When the vegetables have reached the desired consistency (if you like them crispy, this will take 10 minutes), remove the garlic clove, transfer the vegetables onto a serving dish, garnish with basil, and serve. The ratatouille can be served hot or at room temperature, depending on the season.

SAUTÉED VEGETABLES WITH BEAN SPROUTS

Bean sprouts are very easy to digest and are richer in water than soybeans. They also contain more vitamins and minerals, particularly zinc. They help monitor the level of cholesterol and triglycerides in the blood, and also protect capillaries. They help strengthen hair and nails, and fight depression and stress. Their phytoestrogens are believed to act against menopause and osteoporosis.

4 servings
Preparation time: **10 minutes**
Cooking time: **5-10 minutes**
Calories per serving: **150**

3 carrots
1 yellow bell pepper
2 courgettes
2 celery stalks
7 oz. (200 g) bean sprouts
2 tbsp extra virgin olive oil
1 tsp tamari sauce
Salt
Pepper

1. Peel and trim the carrots then cut some into strips and some into chunks. Trim, wash and chop the courgettes. Clean, wash and chop the celery. Wash the pepper, remove the stalk, seeds and white parts, and cut it into small strips. Rinse the sprouts and drain them in a sieve for a few minutes.

2. In a non stick pan, heat two tablespoons of oil and cook the vegetables over medium heat for about 5 minutes, if you like them crispy, or 10 minutes if your prefer them more tender.

3. Right before they're ready, add the bean sprouts and cook for about a minute. Add salt and pepper to taste, but remember you are going to season them later with tamari sauce, which is already quite savoury.

4. Once cooked, transfer the vegetables onto a serving dish, season with tamari sauce, stir and serve.

CAESAR SALAD

Parmesan cheese is an excellent source of energy due to the presence of complete proteins that are easy to digest. It is rich in calcium and magnesium, and also contains traces of other minerals. Despite being of animal origin, about 40% of its fats are unsaturated.

4 servings
Preparation time: **10 minutes**
Cooking time: **5 minutes**
Calories per serving: **250**

1 head Romaine lettuce
1 3/4 oz. (50 g) rice flour
bread
1 3/4 oz. (50 g) sliced bacon
1 oz. (30 g) Parmesan cheese
1 clove of garlic
1 tbsp mayonnaise
Salt
Pepper

1. Clean, wash and dry the lettuce gently. Cut it into strips and wrap it in a damp cloth until ready for use.

2. Peel and finely chop the garlic, then place it in a bowl. Add the mayonnaise and stir.

3. Cut the bread into squares and toast the croutons in a non-stick pan for 3 to 4 minutes, flipping them over several times to prevent them from burning. Use a potato peeler to prepare some Parmesan shavings.

4. Slice the bacon and toast it in a non-stick pan over high heat for 2 to 3 minutes, turning it over several times with a wooden spoon, then transfer it onto a plate to cool.

5. Place the lettuce on a serving dish, add the garlic and mayonnaise dressing, then stir. Season with salt and pepper to taste, then stir again. Now scatter the croutons, the Parmesan shavings and the bacon slices over the salad, and serve.

ICEBERG LETTUCE WITH ORANGE DRESSING

There are many varieties of salad: Romaine, Belgian endive, iceberg, arugula, radicchio, cabbage, cornsalad, watercress and chicory, just to name a few. They are all rich in vitamins A, C and E, as well as antioxidant minerals. They improve digestion, diuresis and evacuation. They increase our sense of fullness and are low in calories. They also help fight the risk of developing cancer, and prevent degenerative and vascular diseases.

EASY

4 servings
Preparation time: **20 minutes**
Resting time: **10 minutes**
Cooking time: **5 minutes**
Calories per serving: **150**

1 head Iceberg lettuce
1 green lemon
2 oranges
1 oz. (30 g) raisins
1 3/4 oz. (50 g) low-fat yoghurt
2 3/4 oz. (80 g) buckwheat flour bread
Salt
Pepper

1. Soak the raisins in warm water for 10 minutes, then drain. Clean, wash and dry the lettuce, then cut it into four. Set it aside until ready for use, wrapped in a damp cloth. Preheat the oven to 400° F (200° C).

2. Wash the oranges and lemon, then slice the latter. Use a vegetable knife to cut the orange peel, the keep it aside until ready for use.

3. Cut the bread into squares and toast it in the oven for about 5 minutes. Take it out and let it cool.

4. Place the raisins, yoghurt, lemon slices and orange peel in a bowl, keeping a few lemon slices and one third of the raisins and orange peel aside as garnish. Season with salt and pepper to taste, then stir. Slice the other orange and arrange the slices around the edge of a few serving dishes, creating a bed on which to arrange the salad. Pour the dressing over the lettuce.

5. Decorate each plate with lemon slices, raisins, and orange peel at will. You can also add some croutons on each plate, or serve them separately.

CRUNCHY PEPPERS

Peppers contain plenty of water (over 90% of their weight), about 1-2% of vegetable protein, 2-3% sugar and only 0.2-0.4% fat. They are a good source of fibres, and also include pectin and different types of cellulose. As a result, these vegetables are ideal for low-calorie diets, have cleansing properties and prevent intestinal diseases. Their vitamin A and C content is high (the latter found in greater quantities than in cabbage and spinach), and both these vitamins are useful antioxidants for the prevention of degenerative diseases.

 EASY

4 servings
Preparation time: **5 minutes**
Cooking time: **10-15 minutes**
Calories per serving: **170**

1. Preheat oven to 400° F (200° C). Wash and dry the peppers, but leave them whole, with the stalk. Coarsely chop the bread.

2. Line a baking tray with greaseproof paper and oil the peppers with your hands, one by one. Arrange them on the greaseproof paper and sprinkle over the breadcrumbs.

3. Bake for 10 to 15 minutes. Keep an eye on the peppers and check that the skin has wrinkled. When you smell that unique, delicious smell of roasted peppers, it means that they're ready.

4. Remove from the oven and let cool for 2 minutes before transferring onto a serving dish. Add salt and pepper to taste before serving.

10 1/2 oz. (300 g) friarielli peppers
10 1/2 oz. (300 g) round peppers
1 3/4 oz. (50 g) millet flour bread
2 tbsp extra virgin olive oil
Salt
Pepper

SAVOURY COURGETTE TARTLETS

Soy cream, a vegetable dressing, is an excellent source of protein, rich in essential amino acids. It also contains fats, carbohydrates and isoflavones, which can reduce the risk of cancer cells forming. The use of soy helps prevent cancer, reduce cholesterol levels, and fight osteoporosis and the symptoms of menopause.

MEDIUM

4 servings
Preparation time: **25 minutes**
Resting time: **60 minutes**
Cooking time: **30 minutes**
Calories per serving: **310**

For the pastry:
3/4 cup (100 g) rice flour
1/3 cup (50 g) corn flour
1/3 cup (50 g) cornmeal
2 eggs
1 oz. (30 g) butter

For the filling:
3 courgettes
3 1/2 oz. (100 g) ricotta
1 egg
4 tbsp (30 g) Parmesan cheese
1/4 cup (50 g) soy cream
Salt
Pepper

1. Preheat the oven to 350° F (180° C). Line four single-serving rectangular baking pans with greaseproof paper. Place the flours on a wooden pastry board, make a well in the centre and break the eggs into the well. Add butter and start mixing the ingredients, keeping in mind that these flours are hard to bind together and that the dough falls apart easily. Therefore, we recommended you combine the ingredients gently, wetting your hands several times. When the dough is smooth, wrap it in cling film and let it rest for at least one hour.

2. Meanwhile, trim, wash and slice the courgettes. Put the ricotta, cream, cheese, egg and courgettes in a bowl, season with salt and pepper to taste, and stir.

3. Flour a work surface with rice flour. With a rolling pin, roll out the dough wafer-thin sheet (approximately 2 mm), then cut four out sheets of the size of the baking pans with a pastry cutter.

4. Arrange the dough in the pans and pour in the filling. Bake for about 30 minutes. While cooking, make sure that the filling becomes firm, and the pastry turns golden brown without burning. If needed, lower the temperature. Once cooked, remove the tartlets from the oven and from the pan. Let cool slightly before serving.

CAULIFLOWER AND BROCCOLI
IN A BÉCHAMEL SAUCE

*Cauliflower is a vegetable rich in minerals such as phosphorus, calcium, potassium, copper and zinc.
It contains vitamins A, C, K and of the B-complex, as well as antioxidants, folic acid and amino acids.
It has strong anti-inflammatory, antibacterial, purifying and mineralising properties. It can also stimulate
the thyroid and regulate blood pressure and the blood pH level.*

MEDIUM

4 servings
Preparation time: **20 minutes**
Cooking time: **10 minutes**
Calories per serving: **250**

10 1/2 oz. (300 g) broccoli
10 1/2 oz. (300 g) cauliflower
2 cups (500 ml) milk
1/3 cup (50 g) corn flour
1 3/4 oz. (50 g) butter
20 g walnuts, shelled
1/2 cup (50 g) millet flour
breadcrumbs
1 tbsp extra virgin olive oil
Salt
Pepper

1. Preheat the oven to 400° F (200° C). Clean, wash and dry the vegetables. Bring a pot filled with plenty of salted water to the boil. Add the vegetables and cook for a minute, then drain and let them cool soaked in cold water and ice, to preserve their bright colour. As soon as they're cold, drain well.

2. In a saucepan, pour the milk, corn flour and butter, add salt and pepper, then stir carefully with a whisk to prevent lumps from forming. Cook over low heat, stirring constantly. When the mixture has thickened and it is soft and creamy, remove the pan from heat.

3. Coarsely chop the walnuts and add them to the breadcrumbs.

4. Grease four single-serving pans. Pour in a layer of béchamel then add a layer of vegetables, and end with another layer of béchamel. Sprinkle over the chopped walnuts and breadcrumbs.

5. Bake for 10 minutes and serve hot.

MINTY AUBERGINES

Garlic can lower blood pressure, improve blood circulation and lower cholesterol. Thus, it helps prevent atherosclerosis and effectively kills germs. Is also provides a high intake of fibre and antioxidants, which fight free radicals and prevent ageing. It contains vitamins C and of the B-complex. Its minerals include calcium, iron, sodium, magnesium, potassium, phosphorus and selenium.

4 servings
Preparation time: **10 minutes**
Cooking time: **4 minutes**
Calories per serving: **300**

2 aubergines
2 cups (200 g) rice flour
breadcrumbs
2 eggs
2/3 cup plus 3 tbsp (200 ml)
olive oil
10 mint leaves
2 cloves of garlic
Salt

1. Gently wash and dry the mint leaves, then set them aside until ready for use.

2. Clean the aubergines, leaving the skin on, and slice them horizontally. Arrange the slices on a chopping board, add salt and tilt the board to drain the excess liquid. Now wash and dry the slices.

3. Break and beat the eggs in a bowl. Put the breadcrumbs in a wide bowl. Now coat your slices: dip them in the egg wash, then roll them in the breadcrumbs, making sure they are fully coated.

4. Heat the oil in a non-stick pan. Crush the garlic and dip it in the oil so that it releases its properties while cooking. When the pan is hot, add the aubergines and fry for 3-4 minutes, flipping over several times with tongs.

5. Place the breadcrumb coated aubergines onto a large plate lined with kitchen paper, to absorb the excess oil. Then transfer them onto a serving dish and garnish with the mint leaves. Serve immediately and sprinkle with salt to taste.

BATTERED ARTICHOKES

Artichokes contain cynarin, a slightly bitter, diuretic substance that aids digestion and is good for the liver. Unfortunately, it is destroyed by cooking. These vegetables are rich in potassium and iron, as well as inulin, a substance that helps reduce cholesterol, and fibres, that help keep the digestive system regular. Artichoke hearts contain antioxidants that can reduce the risk of cancer and vascular diseases.

EASY

4 servings
Preparation time: **10 minutes**
Cooking time: **6-10 minutes**
Calories per serving: **200**

4 artichokes
4 tbsp (30 g) rice flour
4 tbsp (30 g) corn flour
1 glass sparkling water, cold
2/3 cup plus 3 tbsp (200 ml)
peanut oil
Salt

1. Wash and trim the artichokes and snap off the hard, outer leaves, leaving only the soft inner ones. Trim the stem (but leave 3/4 inch/2 cm attached), then soak the artichokes in cold water (slice them at the last moment, as they oxidise easily).

2. Pour the flours and water into a bowl and stir with a whisk until smooth. Slice the artichokes, place them in the bowl with the batter, and mix.

3. Heat the oil in a non-stick pan and wait until it's hot enough for frying (it must reach a temperature of about 340° F/170° C), then add the artichokes and deep fry for 3 minutes, flipping them over several times so as to cook them evenly. Pull the artichokes out with a skimmer and drain off the excess oil on kitchen paper. Repeat with all the artichokes.

4. If you wish, you can cook the remaining batter in oil, pouring it in pools with a spoon. Once ready, remove it from the pan and drain it with the artichokes.

5. Arrange the artichokes and the savoury wafers on a serving dish, add salt to taste and serve immediately.

ROASTED CELERY

Celery contains potassium, calcium, phosphorus, magnesium, selenium and a considerable amount of vitamins A, C and K. Vitamin K is vital to the body's blood coagulation process. This vegetable has purifying and diuretic effects and is a natural stimulant due to its content of aspartic acid, which is why it was once considered an aphrodisiac.

4 servings
Preparation time: **10 minutes**
Cooking time: **35 minutes**
Calories per serving: **270**

4 green celery stalks
2 cups (500 ml) milk
1/3 cup (50 g) corn flour
1 3/4 oz. (50 g) butter
1 cup (100 g) corn flour
breadcrumbs
1 tbsp extra virgin olive oil
Salt
Pepper

1. Preheat the oven to 400° F (200° C). Clean and wash the celery. Bring a pot filled with plenty of salted water to the boil and cook the celery for 5 minutes, then drain.

2. In a saucepan, combine the milk with the corn flour and butter, then add salt and pepper to taste. Stir well, until the mixture is free of lumps. Cook the mixture over low heat, stirring constantly until it has thickened. Use a wooden spoon to prevent it from sticking. When the mixture is creamy, remove the saucepan from the heat.

3. Arrange the whole celery stalks on a greased baking pan then pour the béchamel sauce over them and sprinkle with breadcrumbs.

4. Bake for 20 minutes. Once cooked, remove the celery stalks from the oven and let them cool slightly before serving.

IT IS NOT IMPOSSIBLE TO PREPARE DELICIOUS DESSERTS ELIMINATING WHEAT FLOUR. INDEED, BY CHOOSING OTHER, LESS CONVENTIONAL FLOURS, YOU WILL DISCOVER VALUABLE HEALTH ALLIES WITH A DEFINITE FLAVOR AND TRULY UNEXPECTED CHARACTER.

Is it possible to make biscuits and cakes without using wheat flour? Adopting a new approach to food often requires being strongly motivated or having a particular need: if our child is sensitive to gluten, for example, we will necessarily have to come up with solutions to make cakes, puddings, custards, tarts and muffins made with ingredients that will not jeopardise his or her health.

It is not as difficult as you might think. Hazelnuts, for example, if ground to a powder, are an excellent substitute for flour, and are also much tastier, as well as being packed with nutrients, vitamins and minerals. The same is true for almonds, walnuts, peanuts and all nuts in general. As for chocolate, we are used to considering it in blocks or bars, but powdered it is a good base to be mixed with milk for a delicious pudding, or with eggs, butter and sugar to create crunchy biscuits and cakes that, more often than not, do not require the use of leavening agents. Buckwheat, with its intense flavor and distinctive personality, is also a good substitute for wheat flour, being rich in nutrients. It is especially useful in the preparation of desserts, given the presence of starch, a thickening agent that binds ingredients effectively. Carob also makes an excellent flour, with a very particular flavor reminiscent of chocolate, without however having its stimulating properties. As a result, it is suitable for children and for the elderly – and, of course, for coeliacs, thanks to the total absence of gluten. Basically, there are countless ingredients that can be used to prepare a flour-free dessert. For example, chestnuts can be used to make the traditional Italian castagnaccio, as well as other biscuits and cakes: simply add them to a whole series of other ingredients, and you have a delicious dessert. Corn is another magnificent

DESSERTS

ingredient, with which to create, for example, crunchy biscuits to be dipped in coffee or milk. Millet, which is not much used in Western cooking, is extremely rich in nutrients: higher in protein than wheat and rice, it contains many fibres that help keep the digestive system regular, and has a very unusual flavor, that combines beautifully with pine nuts, for example, and that is even more enhanced when used with honey instead of sugar. The result? Deliciously sweet and balanced desserts, for a well-earned, relaxing break. For gluten-free torcetto biscuits, we can keep the butter and sugar, and simply replace the ground wheat with corn flour and cornmeal. Even muffins are great prepared with a mixture of potato starch and corn flour. As for pancakes, if we use potato starch we can make a soft and smooth mixture that, once cooked, will be light and fluffy, and of the perfect consistency for maple syrup or acacia honey.

VANILLA CUSTARD
WITH CORNMEAL BISCUITS

Vanilla is a fragrant fruit named after the plant on which it grows. Given its intense scent, it is often used to flavor desserts. It has the shape of a long pod and is filled with an oily flesh rich in small seeds. It is high in sugar, fat (about 15%), insoluble fibre and various minerals. Its aromatic properties remain intact even after drying and fermentation.

4 servings
Preparation time: **10 minutes**
Cooking time: **8 minutes**
Calories per serving: **180**

8 cornmeal biscuits
1 tbsp potato starch
2 egg yolks
1/3 cup (70 g) brown cane sugar
1 1/2 cup (400 ml) milk
2 vanilla pods

1. In a small saucepan, bring the milk with the chopped vanilla beans to the boil, cook for 5 minutes over low heat, then strain through a sieve.

2. In a mixing bowl fitted with an electric mixer, whisk the egg yolks with the sugar, until smooth and fluffy.

3. Pour the milk and the potato starch into the egg mixture, then stir. Transfer into a saucepan and let the mixture thicken over low heat, stirring constantly.

4. When the mixture comes to the boil, remove the pan from heat and allow to cool, stirring continuously.

5. Pour the custard into four separate cups and add two biscuits to each cup before serving. You can serve the custard either warm or cold.

TORCETTO BISCUITS WITH POTATO STARCH AND CHESTNUTS

Brown cane sugar is easier to digest than refined white sugar and is rich in vitamins, minerals, fibre and protein. It can be used for a quick intake of glucose and is fat free. As a result, it is suitable as an all-around sweetener, but it is advisable to limit its use to avoid overloading the pancreas.

4 servings
Preparation time: **20 minutes**
Cooking time: **10-15 minutes**
Calories per serving: **450**

1/3 cup (50 g) potato starch
1/3 cup (50 g) chestnut flour
3/4 cup (100 g) rice flour
2 eggs
1 oz. (30 g) butter
3/4 oz. (20 g) milk
1/4 cup (50 g) brown cane sugar

1. Preheat the oven to 400° F (200° C) and line a baking sheet with greaseproof paper. Melt the butter in a double boiler. In a bowl, mix flours, milk, eggs, butter and half the sugar. Knead the ingredients for at least 10 minutes, until smooth and pliable.

2. Scoop a little dough at a time and shape into small sticks 1/2 inch (1 cm) thick and 4 inches (10 cm) long. Roll the dough in your hands or on a cold floured surface (for example a marble counter or a large plate).

3. Seal the edges of the sticks together (think of the shape of a drop or a horseshoe) to create the typical shape of a torcetto biscuit.

4. Sprinkle your biscuits with the remaining sugar, arrange on a baking sheet lined with greaseproof paper and bake for 10 to 15 minutes.

5. Once ready, remove from the oven and allow the biscuits to cool slightly, then transfer to a cookie jar or serve.

BLUEBERRY MUFFINS

Blueberries are rich in anthocyanosides and antioxidants that are useful to protect the eyesight. They also contain hydrocinnamic acid, which is believed to eliminate all carcinogenic substances produced in the digestive tract. Lastly, they are known to prevent capillary fragility and all blood vessel diseases.

MEDIUM

4 servings
Preparation time: **20 minutes**
Cooking time: **20 minutes**
Calories per serving: **280**

3/4 cup (100 g) cornmeal
1/3 cup (50 g) corn flour
1/3 cup (50 g) potato starch
1/4 cup milk
1 egg
1/3 cup (80 g) brown cane sugar
2 tbsp low fat natural yoghurt
1 tsp baking soda
7 oz. (200 g) blueberries
4 muffin paper cups

1. Preheat the oven to 350° F (180 ° C). Mix the flours and milk in a bowl.

2. Using an electric mixer, whisk the egg with the sugar until smooth, then add to the dry ingredients and stir.

3. Pour the yoghurt and baking soda into a separate bowl. When the mixture starts to rise, incorporate it into the flour and egg mixture, then add the freshly crushed blueberries, and stir.

4. Pour the batter into single muffin paper cups. To avoid the batter from spilling while cooking, place the muffin cups into a metal muffin tin and bake for 20 minutes.

5. Once cooked through, remove the tin from the oven and allow to cool completely, then take the muffins out of the tin, but leave them inside the cups. Muffins can be eaten warm, but will taste just as good cold.

CHOCOLATE AND COFFEE KRUMIRI BISCUITS

Coffee is the most popular drink in the world, after tea. In addition to antioxidant bioflavonoids, it contains several stimulants, the most important of which is caffeine. It helps digestion but it is not suitable for those who suffer from various stomach diseases. It can help fight headaches, but can also cause anxiety and insomnia.

HIGH

4 servings
Preparation time: **90 minutes**
Resting time: **70 minutes**
Cooking time: **20 minutes**
Calories per serving: **520**

3/4 cup (100 g) corn flour
3/4 cup (100 g) potato starch
1/2 cup (100 g) brown cane sugar
2 3/4 oz. (80 g) butter
1 egg
2 egg yolks
1/2 vanilla pod
5 oz. (150 g) dark chocolate
1 cup of strong coffee

1. Preheat the oven to 425° F (220° C) and line a baking sheet with greaseproof paper.

2. Soften the butter in a double boiler with the chopped half vanilla pod. Let it stand for about 10 minutes, until the butter absorbs the vanilla scent, then remove the chopped vanilla bean and add the sugar. Stir until smooth and creamy. Now add the egg and egg yolks and beat the mixture using an electric mixer.

3. Pour the flours into a bowl and add the vanilla custard, stirring until smooth and firm. Cover and let stand for an hour in the refrigerator.

4. Transfer the mixture into a pastry bag with a rectangular notched nozzle. Press the bag on the greaseproof paper and shape the batter into a typical krumiri biscuit. Transfer the baking sheet into the oven and bake the biscuits for 10 minutes, then lower the temperature to 350° F (180 ° C) and cook for a further 10 minutes. Remove from the oven and allow to cool completely.

5. Meanwhile, melt the chocolate in a double boiler and add the coffee. Stir until smooth and firm, then dip in each biscuit, and arrange on a sheet of greaseproof paper. Let the biscuits cool in the refrigerator.

HONEY PANCAKES

Acacia honey provides a quick energy boost, which does not require a particular digestive process. It rich in fructose, its main component, but also contains minerals, enzymes and trace elements. It performs an effective gastroprotective action and helps fight Helicobacter pylori.

4 servings
Preparation time: **15 minutes**
Cooking time: **5 minutes**
Calories per serving: **200**

1. In a bowl, pour the milk, starch, eggs and baking powder. Whisk the ingredients until the mixture is smooth and free of lumps.

2. Soak some kitchen paper in oil and brush a non-stick skillet, then heat the skillet on high heat. Using a ladle pour the batter in pools and cook for a few minutes.

3. When the pancakes have bubbles on top and come off easily, flip them over with a spatula and cook on the other side. Continue with the remaining batter.

4. Serve on a platter and pour the honey while the pancakes are still hot.

1/2 cups (400 ml) milk
3/4 cup (100 g) potato starch
1 sachet baking powder
2 eggs
2 tbsp (40 g) acacia honey
2 tbsp olive oil

ALMOND BISCUITS WITH ALMOND MILK

Almonds are high in fibre and are an excellent source of magnesium and vitamin E. These delicious oily fruits also contain other minerals like potassium, phosphorus, zinc and iron, which are essential for mental alertness and creativity.

4 servings
Preparation time: **20 minutes**
Cooking time: **20 minutes**
Calories per serving: **680**

14 oz. (400 g) almond paste
1 oz. (30 g) almonds
1 egg yolk
1/3 cup (50 g) icing sugar

1. Preheat the oven to 425° F (220° C) and line a baking sheet with greaseproof paper.

2. Knead the almond paste until pliable and soft, then shape into balls and place on the baking sheet (keep four balls aside to prepare the almond milk).

3. Press the balls between the palms of your hands, and flatten them slightly. Create a small hole on top of the biscuits and press in one almond.

4. In a small bowl, lightly beat the egg yolk and brush the biscuits. Bake for about 20 minutes; you can reduce the cooking time if you prefer a soft inside or keep the biscuits in the oven if you like them crispy. Once cooked to your liking, remove the biscuits from the oven and allow them to cool at room temperature, then sprinkle with icing sugar.

5. Just before serving, dissolve the remaining almond paste in four separate glasses of cold water, stirring with a whisk. When the mixture is white and lump-free, your drink is ready.

BUCKWHEAT, CORN AND RICE PINEAPPLE CAKE

Pineapple is native to South America and is made up of 90% water. It is rich in vitamin A, C and of the B-complex, as well as amino acids and minerals such as manganese, potassium and phosphorus. It is very good for the skin and contains anti-inflammatory substances such as bromelain, also useful for preventing artherosclerotic plaques.

MEDIUM

4 servings
Preparation time: **20 minutes**
Cooking time: **30 minutes**
Calories per serving: **300**

1/2 cup (50 g) buckwheat flour
1/3 cup (50 g) cornmeal
1/3 cup (50 g) rice flour
1/3 cup (50 g) corn flour
1/4 cup (50 g) low-fat yoghurt
1 tsp baking soda
2 eggs
1/4 cup (50 g) brown cane sugar
1/cup (100 ml) pineapple juice
10 1/2 oz. (300 g) pineapple

1. Preheat the oven to 350° F (180° C). Place the flours in a bowl. Cut the pineapple into thin slices and set aside until needed.

2. Using an electric mixer, beat the eggs with sugar until creamy, then incorporate them into the dry ingredients.

3. Knead for at least 10 minutes, pouring the pineapple juice into the mixture a little at a time in order to soften it and make it more pliable.

4. Put the yoghurt in a bowl, sift in the baking soda, and stir. When the mixture starts rising, combine with the rest of the ingredients.

5. Now pour the mixture into a rectangular cake pan lined with greaseproof paper. Level the surface and arrange pineapple slices on top.

6. Bake for about 30 minutes, reducing or increasing the cooking time according to the desired crispness. Remove the cake from the oven and allow to cool at room temperature, then gently remove from the tin and transfer to a platter before serving.

HAZELNUT CAKE

When used in small quantities, butter has a lower calorie count than olive and seed oil as it contains water. As it is a fat of animal origin, it has a high cholesterol and saturated fat content. It also contains minerals and vitamin A. At the supermarket, always choose farm butter over processed butter.

MEDIUM

4 servings
Preparation time: **20 minutes**
Cooking time: **35 minutes**
Calories per serving: **570**

5 oz. (150 g) toasted hazelnuts, unshelled
1/3 cup (50 g) potato starch
1/2 cup (100 g) brown cane sugar
2 tbsp (30 g) butter
3 eggs
1 lemon
1 sachet baking powder
1 tbsp (20 g) hazelnut oil
1/2 cup (100 ml) milk

1. Preheat the oven to 400° F (200° C). Grate the lemon zest and soften the butter in a bowl at room temperature.

2. Grind the hazelnuts in a mortar until very fine, almost powdery. Then coarsely chop some (6 or 7) of the leftover nuts and use them later as garnish.

3. Break the eggs into a bowl, add the sugar, lemon zest, ground hazelnuts, potato starch and baking powder. Add the butter, hazelnut oil and milk, then stir to combine all the ingredients and until your mixture is smooth, creamy and lump-free.

4. Pour the batter into a cake pan lined with greaseproof paper, gently level the top with a wooden spoon and sprinkle with coarsely chopped hazelnuts.

5. Bake the cake for about 35 minutes, then remove from the oven and allow to cool slightly. Turn it out of the pan and transfer it onto a platter before serving.

MILLET FLOUR CAKE
WITH PINE NUTS

Pine nuts are made up of 50% fats, mainly unsaturated, which improve blood circulation. They contain vitamins A, E, and of the B-complex, as well as many essential amino acids. It is also a good source of minerals, such as phosphorus, copper, selenium and iron.

MEDIUM

4 servings
Preparation time: **20 minutes**
Cooking time: **30 minutes**
Calories per serving: **480**

1 1/4 cup (150 g) millet flour
1/3 cup (50 g) potato starch
1 sachet baking powder
2 eggs
1 3/4 oz. (50 g) farm butter
2 tbsp (50 g) wildflower honey
1 oz. (30 g) pine nuts

1. Preheat the oven to 350° F (180° C) and line a cake pan with greaseproof paper. In order to make the paper stick to the pan, soak it in cold water, squeeze out excess the liquid and then wrap the pan.

2. Let the butter soften at room temperature.

3. In a bowl, sift in the flours and baking powder, then break the eggs and add the softened butter. Add the honey and stir well to combine all the ingredients.

4. Pour the batter into the cake pan, level the top and sprinkle with pine nuts.

5. Bake for about 30 minutes, making sure the cake is cooking evenly, but without opening the oven. When the cake is ready, remove it from the oven and allow it to cool slightly at room temperature, then turn it out the pan and place it on a platter before serving.

JAM TARTLETS

Plums have a high concentration of minerals such as iron, phosphorus, calcium and potassium. They also contain vitamins C, K and of the B-complex, as well as antioxidants and anti-ageing and invigorating substances like quercetin. They have a strong laxative effect, due to the presence of diphenyl-isatin.

MEDIUM

4 servings
Preparation time: **90 minutes**
Resting time: **30 minutes**
Cooking time: **25 minutes**
Calories per serving: **450**

For the pastry:
3/4 cup (100 g) rice flour
3/4 cup (100 g) corn flour
1/4 cup (50 g) brown cane sugar
1 3/4 oz. (50 g) butter
2 eggs
Spray oil for the tartlet moulds

For the filling:
1 lb. 2 oz. (500 g) plums
1 3/4 oz. (50 g) fructose

1. Wash, halve and core the plums, then put them in a saucepan with the fructose and cook over low heat for about an hour. Stir regularly to prevent the jam from sticking. Remove from heat and allow to cool. Preheat the oven to 350° F (180 ° C) and spray four separate tartlet moulds with spray oil.

2. To make the pastry, put the flours, sugar, eggs and butter cubes in a bowl. Knead the ingredients until the dough is smooth, elastic and holds together, then wrap it in cling film and let it stand for 30 minutes.

3. Then, on a floured work surface, roll out the dough with a rolling pin to about 2mm in thickness, and cut it into four squares, the size of your tartlet moulds.

4. Transfer the pastry to the moulds, by pressing on the bottom and up the sides. Divide the jam filling among the tartlets. Use a pastry wheel to cut the remaining dough into strips to decorate the tartlets. Bake for about 25 minutes.

5. When the tartlets are ready and your kitchen is filled with an enticing scent, remove them from the oven. Allow them to cool completely before turning them out of the moulds and serving.

PASTRY WRAPPED APPLES

Red apples are one of the few fruits that do not ferment in the intestine. There are many varieties, all gluten-free and with a low calorie content. These fruits contain A, C, and B-complex vitamins, and can reduce the absorption of sugar, which makes them ideal for coeliacs and diabetics. Raw red apples are an astringent, therefore effective against diarrhoea. Once cooked they become a laxative and can help fight constipation. They can fight cancer and help against cardiovascular and respiratory diseases.

4 servings
Preparation time: **20 minutes**
Resting time: **30 minutes**
Cooking time: **20 minutes**
Calories per serving: **430**

1 cup (150 g) rice flour
1 cup (150 g) corn flour
1/4 cup (50 g) brown cane sugar
1 3/4 oz. (50 g) butter
2 eggs
1 egg yolk
4 red apples

1. Preheat the oven to 350° F (180° C) and line a baking sheet with greaseproof paper. Melt the butter in a double boiler.

2. Wash the apples without drying them, and sprinkle them with one teaspoon of sugar each. Place the egg yolk in a bowl.

3. In a separate bowl, place the flours, sugar, butter and eggs. Mix the ingredients together, making sure they do not separate in the process. When the dough is smooth, wrap it in cling film and let it stand in the fridge for at least 30 minutes.

4. Now take the dough out of the fridge and it roll out on a floured work surface using a rolling pin. Taking an apple as reference, cut the dough into four squares such as to be able to wrap them round the apples fully.

5. Wrap each apple in a sheet of pastry. Use your fingers to press the pastry against the surface of the apple. When all the fruits are wrapped, arrange them on a baking sheet and brush them with the egg wash.

6. Bake the pastry wrapped apples for about 20 minutes. When ready, remove them from the oven and let them cool slightly. Preferably serve hot or warm: when you cut them, they will give off a delicious smell.

ROSE HONEY CHESTNUTS

Rose syrup is an excellent flavoring agent that maintains its fragrance in dishes. It also has anti-inflammatory and soothing properties. Mixed in cold water, it is a good thirst quencher. Dissolved in hot water, it is a perfect cough relief remedy.

4 servings
Preparation time: **20 minutes**
Resting time: **60 minutes**
Cooking time: **15 minutes**
Calories per serving: **230**

1. Shell the chestnuts and cook them in boiling waterand two tablespoons of rose syrup, until soft (about 15 minutes).

2. Strain and allow to cool slightly. When the chestnuts are warm, peel them (removing the bitter brown skin) and place them in a bowl.

3. Drizzle the remaining rose syrup and the honey over the peeled chestnuts. Let them rest for about an hour.

4. When serving, remove the chestnuts from the sauce and arrange them on separate small plates. Serve at room temperature. In addition to being a delicious, healthy and easy to make dessert with which to close any meal, rose honey chestnuts are also perfect with cheese and cold cuts.

1 lb. 2 oz. (500 g) chestnuts
1/3 cup. (100 g) acacia honey
3 tbsp rose syrup

CASTAGNACCIO CHESTNUT CAKE

Chestnuts are the fruit of the chestnut tree that belongs to the Fagaceae family. They are made up of 50% water and contain many vitamins: A, C, D and B-complex. Chestnuts have purifying and tonic properties, due to their high content of sugar, and also perform an antioxidant action. Chestnut flour is gluten-free.

4 servings
Preparation time: **10 minutes**
Cooking time: **30 minutes**
Calories per serving: **380**

5 1/2 cups (500 g) chestnut flour
1 oz. (30 g) walnuts, shelled
3/4 oz. (20 g) pine nuts
1 3/4 oz. (50 g) raisins
3 cups (700 ml) water
2 tbsp extra virgin olive oil
2 sprigs fresh rosemary
Salt

1. Preheat the oven to 400° F (200° C). Soak the raisins in warm water, then drain. Coarsely chop the walnuts and pine nuts in a food processor. Wash and dry the rosemary.

2. In a bowl, sift the flour and add a pinch of salt, then add the water a little at a time, stirring constantly with a whisk until the mixture is smooth and firm. Add the chopped walnuts and pine nuts and the raisins (well drained), then stir.

3. Grease a tart tin with kitchen paper soaked in oil and pour in the mixture. Sprinkle the chestnut cake with rosemary and a thin layer of oil.

4. Bake for about 30 minutes, then check that the surface is thoroughly cooked (the surface will crack). When the chestnut cake looks ready, remove it from the oven and let it cool before serving.

5. You can slice or cut the cake into squares and serve it on a cake tray or inside a covered sugar bowl, in order to preserve the moist texture of this soft cake.

CHOCOLATE SALAMI

Dark chocolate contains caffeine and theobromine, stimulants that act on the nervous system, as well as serotonin (which helps fight depression and facilitates the production of feel-good endorphins) and tyramine, another antidepressant protein. Last but not least, dark chocolate is rich in bioflavonoids with antioxidant properties, such as epicatechin, that can prevent cancer, ageing and vascular diseases.

4 servings
Preparation time: **30 minutes**
Resting time: **3 hours**
Calories per serving: **420**

7 oz. (200 g) dark chocolate
7 oz. (200 g) cornmeal biscuits
2 tbsp (50 g) brown cane sugar
1 3/4 oz. (50 g) butter
4 tbsp rum
3 eggs

1. Soften the butter at room temperature and crush the biscuits in a bowl.

2. Melt the chocolate in a double boiler stirring constantly with a wooden spoon until creamy, then remove it from heat and allow it to thicken, but keep it from hardening.

3. Once the butter is softened, place it in a bowl with the sugar, eggs, chocolate, crushed biscuits and rum. Mix well until smooth.

4. Transfer the mixture onto a sheet of greaseproof paper, wrap it in the paper and shape it into a log, or a "salami". Press, roll and work the wrapped log as if it was clay. Once formed into the desired shape, refrigerate the salami for about 3 hours until firm.

5. When ready, take the salami out of the fridge, slice and serve. Protect it from heat, to keep it from melting or softening and therefore lose its texture.

LAYERED CAROB MOUSSE

The carob bean is the fruit of a tree native to Arabia. Carob flour, milled from the pod of the carob bean, is rich in protein, vitamins and minerals. Similar to chocolate in taste, it has a low fat content and, therefore, is a perfect alternative for those wanting to indulge without going overboard in terms of calories.

MEDIUM

4 servings
Preparation time: **15 minutes**
Resting time: **2 hours**
Cooking time: **5 minutes**
Calories per serving: **240**

1. In a blender, purée the blueberries with half the milk and half the sugar. Pour the mixture into a saucepan, cook over low heat and stir constantly while you add the corn flour. Continue to cook over low heat, stirring constantly, until the mixture thickens, then remove from heat.

2. Combine the remaining corn flour and sugar, then incorporate the remaining milk and carob flour. Continue to stir, and bring this second mixture to a boil over very low heat, then remove from heat.

3. Pour into four glasses, and create three different layers, starting with the carob flour mousse, then adding the blueberry custard and finishing with the former.

4. Refrigerate and let stand for about 2 hours. Before serving, garnish with whipped cream and biscuits. Serve hot.

11/2 cups (400 ml) milk
1/2 cup (50 g) carob flour
1 3/4 oz. (50 g) blueberries,
washed and hulled
1 tbsp corn flour
1 tbsp brown cane sugar

To garnish:
3/4 cup (50 g) vegetable
Whipped cream
8 sesame and honey biscuits

LAYERED STRAWBERRY AND BLUEBERRY MOUSSE

Syrups are water and sugar based solutions. Being concentrates, their sugar content is high, which makes them ideal to add flavor, perfume and colour to any preparation. Strawberry syrup keeps the taste, sweetness and aroma of the fruit unaltered.

MEDIUM

4 servings
Preparation time: **15 minutes**
Resting time: **2 hours**
Cooking time: **5 minutes**
Calories per serving: **140**

500 ml milk
3 1/2 oz. (100 g) strawberries
3 1/2 oz. (100 g) strawberry syrup
1 3/4 oz. (50 g) blueberries
3/4 oz. (20 g) cocoa powder
3 tbsp (20 g) corn flour
1 lemon

1. Hull, wash and dry the strawberries. Blend the blueberries, keeping a few aside as garnish. Grate the lemon zest.

2. Pour the milk into a small saucepan and bring to a boil over very low heat, then add the corn flour and lemon zest, stirring constantly. Stir until the mixture thickens.

3. Transfer the milk into three separate bowls: pour the strawberry syrup in one, the cocoa in the second and the blueberry purée in the third. Choose your favourite flavor, and use more milk for this ingredient. Mix well to blend the milk with all the ingredients.

4. Pour a layer of one of the three mixtures into four glasses, then let them cool in the freezer for 10 minutes. Add another layer using one of the other two mousses, and put it back in the freezer to avoid the mixtures from blending. Pour a last layer using the third mixture and refrigerate for about 2 hours.

5. Then, take the glasses out of the fridge and garnish them with a strawberry and a few whole blueberries.

ALMOND AND BISCUIT MOUSSE

Wildflower honey is mainly made up of water, sugars, proteins, organic acids, minerals, group B and C vitamins, substances derived from flowers (tannins, pigments, phosphate and vitamins) and inhibin, a natural antibiotic. It is high in fructose, and this is very important since fructose is a 100% natural sugar that has not been processed in any way.

MEDIUM

4 servings
Preparation time: **15 minutes**
Resting time: **2 hours**
Cooking time: **5 minutes**
Calories per serving: **380**

1 1/2 cups (400 ml) milk
1 tbsp sugar
1 tbsp corn flour
3/4 oz. (20 g) cocoa powder
3 1/2 oz. (100 g) almond biscuits
3 1/2 oz. (100 g) fresh ricotta
1 tbsp wildflower honey

1. Coarsely crush some biscuits in a food processor or in a mortar.

2. In a small saucepan, boil half the milk and then add half the corn flour, stirring constantly. Bring to the boil over very low heat, allow the mixture to thicken, then remove from heat and allow it to cool slightly. Prepare the chocolate mousse with the remaining milk, blended with the cocoa powder, the remaining corn flour and the sugar. Remember to stir constantly.

3. Once warm, incorporate the ricotta cheese into the first, milk-based mixture, then add the honey and stir.

4. Pour a layer of ricotta and milk mousse into four glasses, then add a layer of biscuits and finally a layer of chocolate mousse. Sprinkle each glass with the remaining crushed biscuits.

5. Refrigerate for about 2 hours, then take the glasses out of the fridge and serve.

INDEX

BIOGRAPHIES

Maurizio Cusani was born in Como and is an ophthalmologist in Milan. Maurizio is interested in the relationship between art, psychology, food and health. To pursue this interest he immersed himself in Sufism and ancient traditions to which he is always attentive, also as an inquisitive traveller. He teaches enneagrams and the symbolism of the human body in naturopathy courses and to Master's degree students of psychosomatics for doctors and psychologists at the Riza institute. He has been deeply interested in food and its repercussions on health for several years. He has written numerous articles on this subject and on nutraceutics, symbolism, Sufism, ancient traditions, psychosomatics and health in general, for various publishers including Riza, Red, Nuova Ipsa and Sagep-La Lontra.

Cinzia Trenchi is a naturopath, journalist and freelance photographer specialising in food and enogastronomic itineraries. She brings new recipes and fresh interpretations of cookery books published by Italian and foreign editors. Cinzia is an enthusiastic cook and has been working for many years with various Italian magazines on reviewing regional specialities, traditions, macrobiotics and natural cooking. She provides both the written word and the photos needed to illustrate her creations. An inquisitive traveller, she always tries out local traditional dishes and re-interprets them to match her own sense of taste. Cinzia writes cookery books providing original and creative dishes. She links tastes and tries unusual flavor pairings to experiment with new tastes and to find new ways of pleasing the palate. She never loses sight however of the nutritional aspects of food, and always aims to achieve a good balance between what is served at the table and what is good for the health. She lives in Monferrato, in Piedmont, in a house surrounded by greenery. She uses flowers, aromatic herbs and vegetables from her garden to prepare sauces and original seasonings, not to mention decorations for her dishes. She only uses produce that is in season and is deftly guided by her knowledge of what nature provides.

WS White Star Publishers® is a registered trademark
property of De Agostini Libri S.p.A.

© 2013 De Agostini Libri S.p.A.
Via G. da Verrazano, 15 - 28100 Novara, Italy
www.whitestar.it - www.deagostini.it

Translation, editing and layout: Soget Srl

ISBN 978-88-544-0757-2
1 2 3 4 5 6   17 16 15 14 13

Printed in China